T0295765

HERMENEUTICS OF CAPITAL

A POST-AUSTRIAN THEORY FOR A KALEIDIC WORLD

ECONOMIC ISSUES, PROBLEMS AND PERSPECTIVES

Additional books in this series can be found on Nova's website under the Series tab.

Additional e-books in this series can be found on Nova's website under the eBooks tab.

ECONOMIC ISSUES, PROBLEMS AND PERSPECTIVES

HERMENEUTICS OF CAPITAL

A POST-AUSTRIAN THEORY
FOR A KALEIDIC WORLD

CARMELO FERLITO

New York

NOTICE TO THE READER

Library of Congress Cataloging-in-Publication Data

Names: Ferlito, Carmelo, author.
Title: Hermeneutics of capital : a post-Austrian theory for a kaleidic world
   / editor, Carmelo Ferlito (INTI International College Subang, Subang Jaya,
   Malaysia, and Institute for Democracy and Economic Affairs (IDEAS), Kuala
   Lumpur, Malaysia).
Description: Hauppauge, New York : Nova Science Publishers, Inc., 2016. |
   Series: Economic issues, problems and perspectives | Includes
   bibliographical references and index.
Identifiers: LCCN 2016017085 (print) | LCCN 2016022543 (ebook) | ISBN
   9781634851299 (softcover) | ISBN 9781634852357 ()
Subjects: LCSH: Capital. | Austrian school of economics.
Classification: LCC HB501 .F4185 2016 (print) | LCC HB501 (ebook) | DDC
   332/.04101--dc23
LC record available at https://lccn.loc.gov/2016017085

Published by Nova Science Publishers, Inc. † New York

CONTENTS

FOREWORD

Neoclassical economics has a theory of capital which leaves much to be desired. Capital is modeled, essentially, as a stock of productive resources used to produce consumer goods and services. But not only is it considered a stock. In the standard model capital is treated as homogeneous, as an upper-case K in an equation. Each element of the capital stock—each "piece," as it were—is considered the same as every other piece, as if the stock of capital was simply a huge lump of stuff, such as putty or clay.

In contrast, the Austrian School has emphasized the heterogeneous nature of capital. Wine barrels (a capital good for a winery) cannot possibly be considered the same thing as a blast furnace (a capital good for a foundry). Each serves quite different purposes, plans, and objectives. Each has a specific use. In this case, one is not a substitute for the other but are used in combination with other capital goods to produce different products.

Rather than a theory of the "stock" of capital, Austrians view capital as a structure, a remarkably complex and ever-changing array of parts (themselves guided by differing investment plans of entrepreneurial profit seekers). The structure must be coordinated through time, in such a way that not only present household consumption plans can be met but future consumption plans as well. Here, market prices that reflect underlying supply and demand conditions and, critically, market interest rates that coordinate household saving and consumption plans become the key to explaining a well-coordinated, growing economy. And, should interest rates be manipulated by a central bank, saving and consumption plans can diverge, relative prices throughout the capital structure can be distorted, and an unsustainable boom could occur, leading to an eventual (and inevitable) bust.

In this book Professor Ferlito seeks to build upon—and move beyond—the traditional Austrian view of capital and its place in an explanation of the business cycle. He calls for a hermeneutics of capital. But just what is hermeneutics? It is certainly a term unfamiliar to about 99 percent of the economics profession.

Hermeneutics is the art of interpretation. Hermeneutics first emerged as a way to interpret the meaning of biblical (and later, legal) texts about two centuries ago, through the approach of Friedrich Schleiermacher. But with the work of Hans-Georg Gadamer in the 1960s, and Paul Ricoeur in the '70s and '80s, hermeneutics as we know it today has come to treat human action itself as a text. It emphasizes that people are interpretive beings. Everyday people face the challenge of interpreting the actions, the meaning, and the plans of others in the social world. On top of that, the social scientist faces the challenge of interpreting the actions and meanings of the agents he himself studies. To understand the meaning of an entrepreneur's actions, for example, the theorist has to understand the plans of the entrepreneur and the way in which the entrepreneur interprets prices, interest rates, and the profit possibilities that might be achieved by combining capital goods in specific ways. Mainstream economists simply haven't bothered to do that, and only a handful of us Austrians have.

Professor Ferlito is one of them, and he does so in a rather subtle way. To explain a complex, dynamic, and growing economy more fully—let alone its breakdown—real time, uncertainty, and entrepreneurial expectations play key roles. For example, prices aren't simply given pieces of data. Prices, and price changes, must be interpreted. Outlays and expenses aren't simply numbers on an accounting spreadsheet. They, too, must be interpreted. (The entrepreneur must ask him- or herself not only why their revenues have fallen, for example, but also what it means for business and how it bodes for the future). Profitable innovation, properly understood, can only occur in real time and under conditions of true uncertainty. It is therefore based upon an interpretive act. So, too, are the countless acts of entrepreneurial imitation that often follow in the wake of successful innovators, who are expecting to profit as well. Indeed, an expectation itself is fundamentally an act of interpretation.

And, tying this directly back to a theory of capital, so, too, is a capital good itself. For capital goods are not "given" in a dynamic economy. An entrepreneur must first employ his imagination and try to determine (or discover) which resources are suitable to serve his profit-seeking purposes. Having formulated his plan, those resources only then become actual capital goods once the plan is put into action.

For Professor Ferlito, the implications of a hermeneutical theory of capital are enormous. He takes the analysis in a direction that the rest of us hermeneutical Austrians, and Austrian fans of Joseph Schumpeter, might not agree upon. Drawing more from Schumpeter's theory of entrepreneurial innovation (and imitation) than from Israel Kirzner's concept of entrepreneurial alertness (which seems to downplay the importance of the interpretive act), Professor Ferlito embarks upon a "Post-Austrian" theory of capital and the boom-bust cycle. He argues that the processes of Schumpeterian innovation and imitation—and especially the speculative excitement that it breeds—could shift a growing economy into a bust . . . without the interest-rate manipulation of a nation's central bank. This challenges the traditional Austrian theory of the business cycle. Post-Keynesian economists, especially those who are influenced by Hyman Minsky's work (who himself employs something of a Schumpeterian dynamic), should also take note.

This book is, indeed, not your traditional Austrian analysis, and it sets the stage for a whole new level of debate.

—*David L. Prychitko*
Department of Economics
Northern Michigan University
Marquette, MI, USA

ENDORSEMENTS

"Building on Ludwig Lachmann's approach, this fascinating and well-written book provides new insights into the philosophical and hermeneutical presuppositions of the Austrian school of economics and explores new directions into fields such as theory of capital, entrepreneurship theory and business cycle theory. Ferlito's book is an excellent piece of work bound to capture the interest of any scholar who considers philosophy to be a more relevant sister discipline to economics than mathematics."

—Francesco Di Iorio
Southeast University, Nanjing, China

"Ferlito develops a theory of capital grounded in how people with imperfect knowledge interpret the real world and over time learn and adjust their actions to it. He tackles head-on the tough, complex issues surrounding the nature and significance of capital and traces with intelligence and determination their game-changing consequences for economic analysis in general and business-cycle theory in particular."

—Sanford Ikeda
Purchase College, State University of New York, Purchase, NY, USA

"Original, accessible and brilliantly written, this book provides a stimulating new reading of the core ideas of Austrian economics: capital, expectations and business cycle. *Hermeneutics of Capital* demonstrates that crises cannot be understood without considering the naturalness of economic fluctuations."

—Stefano Lucarelli
University of Bergamo, Bergamo, Italy

"Hermeneutics of Capital is a must-read book for free-market think tank leaders and academics. Dr. Ferlito reframes the Austrian School of Economics idea of *capital theory* leading us to a new *human oriented* approach where individual intentions and expectations are not the direct result of economic features but the result of human action."

—*Lorenzo Montanari*
Property Rights Alliance, Washington, DC, USA

"The market is a network of millions of companies that complement and coordinate with each other intertemporally and synchronically, forming an extremely complex production structure. In order to understand how and why this structure is coordinated or discoordinated, we need to apply a theory allowing us to study the way it works, that is, a capital theory. However, despite the fact of its importance, economists have systematically ignored neglected such a need and we do not have a developed capital theory. In *Hermeneutics of Capital*, Dr. Carmelo Ferlito faces the challenge of building a modern theory of capital. This is a remarkable book that will change the understanding of many economists on how the market actually works."

—*David Sanz Bas*
Universidad Católica Santa Teresa de Jesús de Ávila, Ávila, Spain

"Carmelo Ferlito, tackling controversial theoretical issues, is able to guide the reader, who does not necessarily need to be an economist, as the reading is easy and immediately understandable; indeed the book is not written for specialists only. To investigate capital theory requires a deep knowledge of analytical tools, imposing a documented speculation, in turn the result of rigorous research and personal evaluations. The author, building on his cultural background, shows high scientific rigor, as indeed also testified by his past and qualified publications."

—*Cristina Spiller*
University of Verona, Verona, Italy

PREFACE

In presenting *Hermeneutics of Capital*, I fear that most modern economists are not prepared or even interested in the approach I take in this book. Today economists are more likely to search for "exact" theories, functional relationships between often logically independent variables rather than to question the nature of their science and its main task. However, as clearly pointed out by Shackle (1972, 24) a "discipline, a region of the world of thought, should seek to *know itself*. Like an individual human being, it has received from its origins to stamp of character, a native mode of response to the situations confronting it. Right responses, 'responsibility,' will require of the profession as of the individual an insight into the powers and defects of the tool which history has bequeathed to it."

Today, faced with the inability of economists to interpret the economic phenomena of our time, I cannot but acknowledge that this is the outcome of the abandonment of self-awareness. Most economists have given up questioning the purposes and the means of their scientific work, seeking refuge on a second line: algebraic analysis of functional relationships. Economics has become econometrics. The result is the formulation of economic theories that are apparently "exact" but nevertheless not true. Not everything that can be proven mathematically is also logically valid. Faced with the difficult economic situation we are experiencing, it is worrying to see that economists, particularly and precisely those who are responsible for economic and monetary policies, are no longer able to say anything meaningful.

This is the outcome achieved by believing that the method of natural sciences, founded precisely on the discovery of universally valid functional relationships, can be applied to economics. This is the result of relegating the question of methodology to a kind of scientific itching for minor intellectuals and meticulous scholars with a mania for philosophy. Consequently, "materialism and the illuminated hunger of 'pure facts' have again witnessed a schism, the unilateral and inorganic assumption of a part of the whole" (Evola 1942, 142). It would therefore be preferable point out that there have to be methodological indications to which an economist must refer, in an attempt to restore dignity to a science by now discredited in many people's eyes. It is not possible to be 'pure' economists; only a wider theoretical vision also allows analysis of theoretical facts. As stressed by Evola (1931, 89), "*knowledge* is universal, when it manages to give us the meaning of things, before whose magnitude and whose eternity, all that is *pathos* and tendency among men disappears: when it leads us to the primordial and cosmic, to what in the field of the spirit has the same characters of purity and power as the oceans, deserts and glaciers."

Certainly, such emotions are not to be found when attempting to read today's econometric texts. Every economic theory can be only part of a more general gnoseological awareness. Such awareness was present in economists of the caliber of Schumpeter, who (1934, 3) explained how the "social process is really one whole indivisible. Out of its great stream the classifying hand of the investigator artificially extracts economic facts. The designation of a fact as economic already involves an abstraction, the first of many forced upon us by the technical conditions of mentally copying reality. A fact is never exclusively or purely economic; other—and often more important—aspects always exist. Nevertheless, we speak of economic facts in science just as in ordinary life, and with the same right; with the same right, too, with which we may write a history of literature even though the literature of a people is inseparably connected with all the other elements of its existence."

In the wake of Shackle (1953, 244–245), this book will argue that "economics is about human nature, human conduct and human institutions," what Mises (1949) called *human action*. Therefore economics focuses on what Menegazzi (1970, 21) called *vital phenomena* "which are proven to exist but whose intimate mystery has not been revealed. Most people accept that the unexplored world is boundless and that traditional scientific methods, despite their continuous transformation, do not suffice for attaining the truth." As we shall see in the following chapters, it is the purpose, the expectation that determines the action—and precisely the opposite of what happens for natural phenomena. Vitalistic theories "reaffirm, as a characteristic principle of life, the *principle of finality* [...]. It appears that this thinking the links to the finality outlined by the Aristotelian-Thomistic school, reveals [...] how the vital phenomenon involves "a *reversal of the causal relationship*. [...] In the physical-chemical world, there is nothing that would even remotely resemble this self-regulating capacity of living beings. *In a mechanism, the result depends on the process; in an organism, on the contrary, the process depends on the result: a guiding and unifying entity is manifested that transcends every possible experiment: it is the principle of life*" (Menegazzi 1970, 35).

So far, instead, economics evolution has ignored two fundamental characteristics of human action, i.e., unpredictability and freedom. These aspects impose serious limits on possibilities for theorizing and prediction in the sphere of economics. The desire to apply the methods of natural sciences to human sciences generates the perverse effect of identifying presumed functional relationships of a mathematical nature. Yet this is not possible. This faulty belief gave rise to the theoretical artifice of general equilibrium theory, a constructivist tool that is actually rather pointless for economists having a sincere interest in reality.

Economists are faced by qualitatively very well defined elements: man and reality. They should be inspired by these elements, should—I would add—allow themselves to be astonished by what happens. The essence of an economist's work lies in observation of reality, without seeking to put it in a cage. Observation of reality helps identify certain dynamic trends that represent constants in human action. For example, as we have seen, the human action has a finalistic nature. That is not to say, as in the rationalist terms of the general equilibrium theory, that every subject maximizes units of utility in accordance with mathematical models. This is not what happens in reality. It is true, however, as a dynamic trend, that man acts to achieve goals, to achieve desires. This sees the onset of relationships with the surroundings, people, things, and complex society in general. Economists may certainly analyze everything that individuals do within the dynamics of enterprise in the search to attain their objectives.

This definition may seem extraneous to more familiar concepts in economics such as prices, interest rates, profit and loss, and the like. But this is not the case. As we will see later, when defining their goals, people also choose the means for achieving them. In doing so, the attainment of other goals is waived, and this becomes the cost of the action. If the goal is reached within the desired terms, and the satisfaction achieved is superior to the waiver, then the outcome is positive. Prices, in numerical terms, are merely a brief representation of subjective assessments and their variegated universe. In the course of their actions, individuals meet each other, and, unconsciously, their assessments of ends and means meet in turn and start an unending journey of mediation. The market comes into being as a spontaneous institution, a place for relationships, where the individual choice over means and ends is challenged through interrelationships. The system of prices emerges in this process as the mediated (objective) result of the combination of subjective assessments. This system of values allows those involved to make rational economic calculations and verify, over time, whether they are attaining their goals or not.

The methodology which I described so far is the one developed by the Austrian School of Economics (ASE), which I belong to, following its first appearance with Menger (1871). The present book, however, is not an epistemological one. It is about *capital theory*. Capital theory is one of the most controversial topics inside the ASE, as it will be briefly explained in Chapter 1; if Böhm-Bawerk capital theory, usually identified as the Austrian Theory of Capital (ATC), left many Austrian economists unsatisfied, a clear definition of capital, consistent with Mengerian subjectivism, is still to be seen inside the school, though important contributions by Hayek, Lachmann, and, more recently, Garrison and Lewin tried to fill the gap. Capital theory seems to be at odds with the role of human action as we described it above. The attempt of *Hermeneutics of Capital* is to reconcile man and capital, which are often presented as competing elements in a conflictual world. What I tried to do is even more than looking for a simple reconciliation; following Ludwig Lachmann's application of hermeneutics to economics, I tried to define capital as the outcome of subjective mental processes, determined by individual intentions and expectations and not by specific physical or economic features. Thus Chapter 1 does not aim to redefine *capital theory* totally but, more specifically, to reach a definition for *capital*, *capital goods*, and *capital value*; such definitions try to complete the work initiated by Lachmann (1956), and my hope is that they could find a certain consensus among scholars dissatisfied with the present state of capital theory, dominated by an objectivist post-Ricardian perspective.

As mentioned in the subtitle of the book, I define my theory post-Austrian. In fact, though recognizing myself as member of the ASE, my attempt is to further develop it, trying to contribute by enhancing concepts and theories which I believe need to be reshaped. If in Chapter 1 I tried to bring at conclusion Lachmann's hermeneutical approach on capital, in Chapter 2 I connected my capital theory with a consistent entrepreneurship theory, which goes beyond the usual contraposition between Kirzner's and Schumpeter's entrepreneurial theories and builds a synthesis centered on the idea of entrepreneurship as a subset of Misesian action involving specific capital formation processes. Finally, in Chapter 3 I took in account the traditional version of the Austrian Business Cycle Theory (ABCT), and I critically revised it; my vision, as previously argued in Ferlito (2013, 2014, 2015c), is that crises are not simply the consequences of monetary manipulations, but they are the natural consequence of every expansionary wave. I distinguished, therefore, between the monetary cycle (as typically described by Mises) and the natural cycle, a cycle in which the boom begins in a way that the traditional ABCT would call sustainable but that, I argue, is followed by a readjustment crisis anyway; to bring out mp point, I integrated the ABCT with Schumpeterian imitation and speculation processes and with the Lachmann's accent on the role of expectations. Also the theory outlined in Chapter 3 is then connected with *capital* definitions brought out in Chapter 1, in order to analyze capital behavior during cyclical movements.

In conclusion, I would like to thank the people who made this book possible. First of all, my wife, Meilina, and my son Elio Paolo: their patience tolerated the time I stole them in order to complete this latest scientific work. Professor Cristina Spiller deserves a special mention because of the continuous trust and support to my academic efforts; her affection played a big role in convincing me not to totally abandon the research activity. A big thanks has to be reserved for some scholars who took the time to read and discuss my work, helping my vision to take shape and improve: above all David Prychitko, an inspired and inspiring disciple of Ludiwig Lachmann, who honored me with a highly appreciated foreword for the present book; then Sanford Ikeda, Stefano Lucarelli, David Sanz Bas, Francesco di Iorio, Emile Phaneuf, Lorenzo Montanari and, in particular, Francesco Meacci, who wisely guided me to a deeper understanding of the different facets of the ATC. I would like to thank the Institute for Democracy and Economic Affairs (IDEAS) in Kuala Lumpur, for giving me the possibility to talk about the Austrian School of Economics widely in Malaysia, and my students at INTI International College Subang, in particular the ones who joined the Friedrich A. von Hayek Institute Malaysia, for confirming me in the consciousness that my academic effort has a bigger meaning.

Shackle (1953, 257) reminded us that a "good economist is like a bottle of wine. He must begin by having the luck to be laid down, as it were, in a vintage year, when he himself and his class companions are the high-quality stuff in which ideas and theories ferment and discourse sparkles in a glow of golden light. But this is not enough. He must mature." I am sure I am not a completely mature economist; my greatest hope is this book is a further step on the maturation path and a help for the readers to understand reality.

Chapter 1

FOR A HERMENEUTICAL DEFINITION
OF CAPITAL

1. HERMENEUTICAL PROCESSES IN TIME:
OUR FRAMEWORK

Ludwig M. Lachmann (1906-1990) was a German economist who studied with Hayek at the London School of Economics during the 1930s.[1] A professor in economics in South Africa and New York, he became, with Israel Kirzner and Murray N. Rothbard, one of the protagonists of the Austrian economics revival during the period 1974-1976.[2] Working on the importance of expectations and the impossibility for the economic system to reach an equilibrium position,[3] even if equilibrating forces are always at work, he gave birth to the "radical subjectivist"[4] stream inside the Austrian school of economics, characterized by the shift from preferences to expectations and by the introduction of hermeneutics in economics[5]. As recalled by Prychitko (1995a, 3)—

> Lachamnn attempted to reconstruct the individualist phenomenology of the Austrian School. He called for a hermeneutical-interpretative project that can study and understand the coordinating roles of social and

---

[1] For a biographical sketch see Mittermeier (1992) and Moss (2000).
[2] See Blundell (2014) and Vaughn (1994, 92–111).
[3] Garrison (1986) opposed Lachmann's 'equilibrium-never' position to Lucas's 'equilibrium-always' approach.
[4] See Koppl and Mongiovi (1998).
[5] Lachmann (1990). See also Di Iorio (2015a, 15–22).

economic institutions. Lachmann was the first economist that I am aware of to suggest that hermeneutics could be profitably applied to economics, particularly as practiced with the Austrian tradition.

Even if he found important followers,[6] Lachmann attracted a strong criticism by Rothbard (1989, 1992),[7] which was mitigated by the so-called Kirznerian middle ground.[8]

The present book, *Hermeneutics of Capital*, is titled after those tradition and it is now necessary to clarify what I have in mind when I talk about the application of hermeneutics to economics in general and to capital theory in particular. Without a doubt, we owe to the Austrian School of Economics (ASE) the idea that human action is the core of economic analysis, a vision directly descending from the subjective revolution initiated by Menger (1871) and culminated in Mises (1949, 92), who clearly stated that economics "is not about things and tangible material objects"; on the contrary, "it is about men, their meanings and actions. Good, commodities, and wealth and all the other notions of conduct are not elements of nature; they are elements of human meaning and conduct. He who wants to deal with them must not look at the external world; he must search for them in the meaning of acting men."

Introducing the category of *meaning* we enter the world of interpretations, *verstehen* (understanding),[9] which is central to the analysis of human action (Antiseri 2011, 7) and which is the most important novelty introduced by Lachmann and his followers.[10] Indeed, *interpretation* processes have to be

---

[6] See in particular Lavoie (1990), Prychitko (1995b) and Rizzo (1979). See also O'Driscoll and Rizzo (1985).

[7] For the debate Lachmann-Rothbard on hermeneutics and disequilibrium see also Rizzo (1992), Boettke, Horwitz, and Prychitko (1986), Selgin (1988), Prychitko (1994; 1995a, 4) and Antiseri (2011).

[8] Kirzner (1992, 3–54; 2000, 132–148). See also Prychitkco (1994, 305).

[9] "Verstehen, i.e., the idea that the ultimate causes of social phenomena must be sought in the meanings individuals attach to their actions and which result from mental interpretative processes" (Di Iorio 2015b, 178).

[10] According to Prychitko (1994), Lachmann introduced a sort of objectivistic hermeneutics, rooted in the Weberian concept of verstehen and focused on the analysis of individual plans in the context of evolving institutions (see, in particular, Lachmann, 1971). Prychitko (1994) argued that such vision is not as radical as Gadamer's and Ricoeur's phenomenological hermeneutics; in Prychitko (1994) the differences between the two approaches are explained at length. However, Antiseri (2011) and Di Iorio (2015a) do not agree with this categorization. According to Di Iorio (2015a, paragraphs 2.3 and 2.4), Gadamer defended an objective conception of truth (similar to the Weberian one), stressing that an interpretation validity is never arbitrary nor subjective, and during the last years of his life he pointed out several common features between his vision and the Popper's that an interpretation validity is never arbitrary nor subjective. Following Popper, Antiseri (2011)

seen as the necessary and subjective link between different objective facts and events. Human actions are objective facts; they are answers to other objective facts, constituting the elements of reality. However, the way in which such answers are defined is totally subjective, the outcome of interpretation processes, which we can define as hermeneutical actions. As explained by Bellet and Durieu (2004, 236), "the relationship between objective economic variables or 'business situations' and expectations depends on the interpretation which the agents give to the former." This is what Lachmann called the subjectivism of active minds. Such a perspective does not deny the objective nature of reality; however, the nature of the response to objective elements is exquisitely subjective, ontologically hermeneutical. An example will help in clarifying my point of view. An earthquake is an objective fact. However, can we say that, economically speaking, the consequences of an earthquake are defined by the earthquake *per se*? If the answer is 'yes,' we must conclude, as modern econometricians try to do, that every earthquake will bring out a certain set of economic consequences, independently from the conditions of time and space, and, above all, independently from the perception generated in the people affected by the natural disaster. We believe, instead, that the answer must be "no." Such an objectification (mechanization) of reality does not take in account the action of real human beings, which takes place as consequence of hermeneutical processes in a specific context of space and time. In fact, a natural disaster can bring out different outcomes. People living in the affected area could react thinking that, even if earthquakes cannot be avoided, it is time to rebuild the town with better engineering techniques, so as to leave future generations a better heritage and to suffer less damages in case of future disasters; in this case, the earthquake would bring out research, investment, general development. But if the disaster is interpreted as a sign that world end is imminent and nothing can be done in order to appease God's anger, then the affected human community would simply stands still, waiting for the unavoidable outcome of an unchangeable destiny. It is clear that the economic consequences of the same event can be radically different, according to the hermeneutical process following the objective fact. The difference lies in processes happing into human minds; of course, such processes are affected by environmental and space-time conditions; however, to be affected does not mean to be objectively determined. The objective outcome is always the result of subjective processes of evaluation and interpretation.

---

explained that fallibility and hermeneutics are different words to describe the same kind of knowledge theory. See also Di Nuoscio (2014).

It is now clear how subjective hermeneutical processes constitute the necessary link between objective facts. Without the interpretative moment, reality could not take shape because no action would be decided. Such a vision explains also the weakness of modern day economics and its focus on economizing and maximizing functions (as described in Robbins's *Essay on the Nature and Significance of Economic Science*).[11] Economizing men (*homo oeconomicus*) make decision with respect to *given* series of ends and means (Kirzner 1973, 32–33): Their action is reduced to reaction. Pareto's agent does not choose his tastes and preferences (Prychitko 1994, 304). The important point raised up by Kirzner is that, in an analytical framework, in which ends and means are given, there is no room to study *how* ends and means are decided. Instead, being

> [. . .] broader than the notion of economizing, the concept of human action does not restrict analysis of the decision to the allocation problem posed by the juxtaposition of scarce means and multiple ends. The decision, in the framework of the human–action approach, is not arrived at merely by mechanical computation of the solution to the maximization problem implicit in the configuration of the given ends and means. It reflects not merely the manipulation of given means to correspond faithfully with the hierarchy of given ends, but also *the very perception of the ends-mean framework* within which allocation and economizing is to take place. (Kirzner 1973, 33).

While Robbins's economizing man can only react, in a given way, to a strictly defined set of ends and means, the Misesian *homo agens* can *also* identify which ends to strive for and which means are available. This is possible because we actually "can *imagine* the future, even a nonexistent, unknowable future" (Kirzner 1992, 25). Instead, economizing behavior does not take into account the process to identify ends and means. At this point the hermeneutical processes described above come into play. How are ends and means actually defined? As Lachmann pointed out, one of the most important achievements of modern subjectivism is the shift from preferences to expectations. An analysis of human action unable to deal with expectations would be maimed. Individual action takes place in a context which generates, via hermeneutical processes, expectations about the future. It is according to such expectations that human minds define their set of ends and corresponding

---

[11] For an earlier and detailed contraposition of Robbinsian economizing agent and Misesian homo agens see Kirzner (1960, 108–185).

means, thought to be adequate to achieve ends. Human action consists of actual implementation of plans, the utilization of means to reach goals defined by the expectations generated by interpretative processes, in turn sprouting from the impact between human beings and surrounding reality.[12] To understand the actions of individuals, it is necessary to reduce action to plan (Koppl 1998, 63).

Such plans implementation happens *in time*. As already clearly pointed out by Menger (1871, quoted in Cowan and Rizzo 1996, 329), the "idea of (originary) causality . . . is inseparable from the idea of time. A process of change involves a beginning and a becoming, and these are only conceivable as processes in time." A suitable concept of time, which will be crucial for my analysis of capital, needs to be introduced. As explained by Meacci and Ferlito (2016), there are indeed two ways of looking at the phenomenon of time, belonging to what Hicks called *economics of time* as distinct from *economics in time*. Those two ways of implementing the role of time in economics may be summarized by saying that time plays in the first case the role of an *ingredient* of the economic process while in Hicks's it rather plays the role of a *container* in which the unwinding of that process is set. Modern Austrian economists built mostly on a Hicksian path, centred on the development of an economics *in* time, linked with the concepts of human actions, expectations, and uncertainty.

As very well explained in Meacci (2006), different conceptions of time gave birth, in economics, to different paradigms: the General Equilibrium Theory (GET paradigm) and the Economics of Uncertainty and Expectations (EUE paradigm).[13] Such a distinction is built on Shackle's (1965)[14] and

---

[12] This is what is usually labelled as the purposefulness of human action. See Cowan and Rizzo (1996, 333–335) and Phaneuf and Ferlito (2014, 159–176).

[13] The following table, from Meacci (2006, 3–4), clarifies the Robinson's distinction between logical and historical time, as summarized in Harris (2005).

	Logical Time	Historical Time
Directionality of time	Reversibility	Irreversibility
Time intensity of action	Instantaneous	Discreteness, lags; inertia
Expectations	Self-realizing, correct foresight	Falsifiable, future unknowable
Information/Knowledge	Complete, free, symmetric	Imperfect, costly, local learning
Capital goods	Substitutability	Specificity, lumpiness
Investment	Elastic	Inertia, driven by animal spirits
Technical change	Disembodied	Embodied, path-dependent
Money/finance	Barter, passive money, complete futures markets	Active money, liquidity preference, incomplete markets

[14] Time of mechanism versus time of uncertainty, or expectational time.

Robinson's (1974)[15] attempts to go beyond a spatialized concept of time in economics, used by neoclassic economists, and move back to a more realistic use of the concept of time. O'Driscoll and Rizzo (1985) distinguished *real time* from *Newtonian time* and linked the first one to the inevitable ignorance that characterizes the process of human action. From Hayek onward Austrians clearly moved into the *historical time* ground, which is vehicle of novelty and source of uncertainty. What O'Driscoll and Rizzo (1985) called *real time* is a further evolution of the Robinsonian historical time and of Shackleian *expectational time*. Mainstream economics, on the contrary, unfolds its theory in a logical time context, what O'Driscoll and Rizzo (1985, 82) defined as *Newtonian time*, a spatialized time, in which "its passage is represented or symbolized by "movements" along a line. Different dates are then portrayed as a succession of line segments (*discrete time*) or points (*continuous time*). In either case, time is fully analogized to space, and what is true of the latter becomes true of the former." O'Driscoll and Rizzo (1985, 82-85) emphasised that time conceived in this way has three main characteristics: homogeneity, mathematical continuity, and causal inertia. Homogeneity means that different temporal moments are simply points in space, a temporal position; nothing may happen between one moment and another. This means that homogeneous time is fundamentally static. Mathematical continuity, on the other hand, implies that time is simply a sequence of moments, which may even be different, but no change can take place endogenously. Since time is a sequence of static situations, each change must be exogenous. Causal inertia, lastly, means that nothing happens with the flow of time. There is no learning, there is no change in knowledge or adjustment of expectations. The system itself must already contain all the elements needed for it to function. It is evident that while such a concept may fit the description of physical phenomena, where actions are always met by the same reactions, it lends itself poorly to representing unpredictable and dynamic human actions.

What interests us, on the other hand, is real time, a "dynamically continuous flow of novel experiences [. . .]. We cannot experience the passage of time except as a flow: something new must happen, or real time will cease to be" (O'Driscoll and Rizzo 1985, 89). As described by O'Driscoll and Rizzo (1985, 89–91), the characteristics of real time are precisely opposite to those of Newtonian time. They are, dynamic continuity, heterogeneity, and causal efficacy. If we consider dynamic continuity, time must consist of *memory* and *expectations*, i.e., it is *structurally* related moments, past and future, through

---

[15] Logical time versus historical time.

the perceptions of the individual; one cannot imagine a present without memory of the past and expectations for the future; consequently, all the moments in the flow of time are intimately linked and reciprocally influenced. Heterogeneity, on the other hand, means that in each successive moment the individual's perception has of the facts may be, and in fact is, different: the past, once it has occurred, becomes memory, enhancing the present and thereby also changing perception of the future; therefore, the perception of things changes from moment to moment, thereby making the characteristics of a given moment in time radically different from those of the previous moment. The direct consequence of heterogeneity is causal efficacy; the flow of time modifies knowledge, awareness, and information, thereby expanding the creative potential of human action. Yet this is possible precisely because of acquisitions made "beforehand" in time.

It is therefore clear that in a context of logical/Newtonian time nothing happens between the moment in which expectations are formed and the moment in which plans are accomplished. Time is just a fiction to distinguish between two different situations, but no obstacles enter the scene to deviate the course of action. However, reality works in a different way. When we allow real/historical time to be part of the analytical framework, then the picture changes radically; we move from a scenario in which *nothing* happens between two objective events to a new situation in which *everything* can happen *continuously*. We have seen how the impact between human beings and reality generates hermeneutical processes through which individuals form their expectations. In turn, expectations define ends and corresponding means; human action, then, consists in the implementation of plans thought to be suitable to achieve ends with the chosen means. At the very first moment in which plans are implemented, however, individuals embark on a process of mutual interaction and further contact with the surrounding reality. Such interaction is a discovery process, revealing to economic actors fundamental information about each other, expectations, ends/means frameworks, and plans. Synthetically, information is transmitted.

Information transmission is another fundamental element for our analytical scheme. Mainstream economics usually moves into a perfect knowledge, a perfect foresight context: information is given once and forever. Introducing human action and historical time, instead, we must move on a ground characterized by imperfect and ever changing knowledge. If information is continuously transmitted and knowledge content therefore correspondently changes, hermeneutical processes need to always be in motion. Novelty and uncertainty brought out by information through the flow of historical time continuously trigger interpretative analyses, with consequent revisions of expectations, ends, means, and plans. What emerges is Shackle's (1972, 76–79) *kaleidic society*, "a society in which sooner or later unexpected change is bound to upset existing patterns, a society "interspersing its moments or intervals of order, assurance and beauty with sudden disintegration and a cascade into a new pattern" (Lachmann 1976d, 54). At the root of such disintegration we find the endless stream of hermeneutical processes through which individuals deal with the continuous flow of novelty due to human action unfolding in a context of *real time*.

2. HERMENEUTICS OF CAPITAL

2.1. Lachmann's Critics to Böhm-Bawerk

This is not the place where to summarize the Austrian Capital Theory (ACT), as developed in particular by Böhm-Bawerk (1884 and 1889).[16] However, in order to reach our *hermeneutical* definition of capital, it is necessary to explain the general feeling of uneasiness raised by Böhm-Bawerk's perspective inside the new generation of Austrian economists, who noticed how such capital theory seemed to part the original Mengerian subjectivist approach and to remain entangled inside neo-Ricardians fences.

In Frank Fetter,[17] at the beginning of the twentieth century, several critics to Böhm-Bawerk's capital theory can already be found. However, it is with Schumpeter that an "attack" on Böhm-Bawerk's approach clearly started, faulting it as not consistent with the Austrian subjectivist paradigm. Elegant as usual, Schumpeter did not directly accuse his former teacher, but he reported what Menger supposedly told him once.[18]

---

[16] On this see in particular Hennings (1997).

[17] See in particular the collection of papers in Fetter (1977).

[18] Also Hayek (1934, 27–28) referred to Mengerian negative position about Böhm-Bawerk's capital theory: "It is pretty certain that we owe this article [Zur Theorie des Kapitals, 1888] to the fact that Menger did not quite agree with the definition of the term capital which was implied in the first, historical part of Böhm-Bawerk's *Capital and Interest*. The discussion is not polemical. Böhm-Bawerk's book is mentioned only to comment it. But its main aim is clearly to rehabilitate the abstract concept of capital as the money value of the property devoted to acquisitive purposes against the Smithian concept of the "produced means of production." His main argument that the distinction of the historical origin of a commodity is irrelevant from an economic point of view, as well as his emphasis on the necessity of clearly distinguishing between the rent obtained from already existing instruments of

[. . .] Menger, far from welcoming that theory [Böhm-Bawerk's one] as a development of suggestions of his, severely condemned it from the first. In his somewhat grandiloquent style he told me once: 'The time will come when people will realize that Böhm-Bawerk's theory is one of the greatest errors ever committed.' He deleted those hints in his 2nd edition. (Schumpeter 1954, 814fn).[19]

Ludwig Lachmann (1976a, 27) explicitly referred to Schumpeter's lines in judging the ACT inadequate for inclusion in the Austrian paradigm.[20] As pointed out by Schumpeter (1954, 813)[21] too, Lachmann stressed that Böhm-Bawerk's analysis was unable to disengage itself completely from the influence of Ricardo. Lachmann's "*j'accuse*" focused in including Böhm-Bawerk's approach into what he called the neo-Ricardian perspective, characterized by *macro-economic formalism*, an analysis conducted "within the context of *macro*-economic equilibrium" (Lachmann 1973a, 14), in which the origins of the motion of the forces of the economic system are systematically ignored.

The German economist included Böhm-Bawerk's approach in what he (1973a, 16) called a *macro-economic formalism* attitude: working exclusively with macro aggregates (Lachmann 1976b, 152) and ignoring the microfoundations (Lachmann 1976c). As Lachmann (1973a) stated in referring to the neo-Ricardian revolution started with Sraffa and Joan Robinson, for them there is no room for subjectivist analysis. They did not focused on the analysis of human action, but of human reaction. According to the Ricardian perspective, individuals are divided into social classes, and real human beings are confined into stereotyped behavior, so that imaginary "beings take the place of real people" (Lachmann 1973a, 18).

---

production and interest proper, refer to points which, even to-day, have not yet received quite the attention they deserve."

[19] See also Gloria-Palermo and Palermo (2004) and Meacci and Ferlito (2016).

[20] See also Lachmann (1973b, 253): "Certainly Böhm-Bawerk was a Ricardian capital theorist who asked questions about the causes and magnitude of interest Ricardo had been unable to answer."

[21] "The Böhm-Bawerkian theory of interest and, incidentally, the Böhm-Bawerkian period of production are only two elements in a comprehensive model of the economic process, the roots of which may be discerned in Ricardo and which parallels that of Marx. [. . .] There is thus a Ricardian root to Böhm-Bawerk's achievement though he was entirely unaware of it." (Schumpeter 1954, 813)

2.2. Austrian Definitions of Capital

Following Lachmann's insights and trying to link themselves back with Menger, next generations of Austrian economists tried to overcome Böhm-Bawerk's contradictions and to develop a subjectivist view on capital. However, what I believe to be still missing in the context of the ACT is a clear definition of what capital is in physical terms and in value.

Surely, some attempts to reach a definition were done, but they seem to remain uncompleted. Menger (1871) simply distinguished between first- (or lower-) order goods, which can directly be used to satisfy needs, and higher-order goods, which needs to be transformed in order to produce lower-order goods and therefore participate only indirectly in the needs satisfaction process; lower- and higher-order goods are related through production processes implemented in time. Rothbard (1962) and Huerta de Soto (2000) worked on such distinction, pointing out that the combination of natural resources, work (human action) and time generates capital goods (Rothbard 1962, 47; Huerta de Soto 2000, 46), which then can be defined as "the intermediate stages of each action process" (Huerta de Soto 2000, 46). They are the Mengerian higher-order goods (Menger, 1871, 58–67), distinguished by the fact of not having immediate consumption as their purpose (Rothbard 1962, 47).

As pointed out by Menger, in order to obtain higher-order goods it is necessary to initiate time-consuming production processes, which, in turn, require *saving* to be implemented (Horwitz 2000, 44; Huerta de Soto 2000, 47; Rothbard 1962, 53). Specifically, in order to obtain capital goods, which require time and resources, immediate consumption of certain resources has to be renounced so that they can be used in a process which will bring about a result over a given period of time. Consequently, without saving (foregoing immediate consumption of certain resources) and without the flow of time (saving must have a certain duration in order to complete the production process) capital cannot exist (i.e., it is not possible to start and finish the process that transforms resources).

Having so described capital goods and capital formation, Huerta de Soto (2000, 50) defined capital as "the market value of capital goods." It seems to me that such descriptions and definitions cannot go in the direction indicated by Menger. I would expect to find a better insight in Lachmann (1956), but the definition presented there also looks disappointing:

> As yet we have left the concept of Capital undefined. We now define it as the (heterogeneous) *stock of material resources*. [...] When capital is defined, with Boehm-Bawerk, as the 'produced means of production' land is, of course, excluded. But to us the question which matters is not which resources are man-made but which are man-used. Historical origin is no concern of ours. Our interest lies in the uses to which a resource is put. In this respect land is no different from other resources. Every capital combination is in fact a combination of land and other resources. (Lachmann 1956, 11)

While Lachmann was able to develop a meaningful critique of capital theories developed inside and outside the Austrian school, introducing the hermeneutical approach as interpretative key for a new way to do economics, he failed to develop a definition of capital consistent with his own insights. It is true that, reading between the lines, we can see the direction Lachmann wanted to follow on capital theory, but a clear alternative statement, able to go beyond Böhm-Bawerk and building on Menger, is still to be found. Similarly, the two Austrians who worked more from a Lachmannian position regarding capital theory, failed to give clear definitions: Garrison (2001) focused on the analysis of capital as structure, while Lewin (2011) preferred to stress the role of capital in a context of disequilibrium. Similarly, Kirzner (1966) confined himself into methodological borders, explicitly refusing to give capital a definition. Therefore, a clear definition of capital is still waiting to emerge.

2.3. A Post-Austrian Definition for Capital and Capital Goods

My aim here is to fill that gap, defining *capital* both in physical terms and in terms of value. Following Menger (1871, 53), we can define *useful* those things "that can be placed in a causal connection with the satisfaction of human needs"; if "we both recognize this causal connection, and have the power actually to direct the useful things to the satisfaction of our needs, we call them *goods*." Menger (1871, p. 53) clearly identified four prerequisites that need to be present simultaneously in order for a thing to acquire the status of a *good*:

1) A human need;
2) Such properties as render the thing capable of being brought into a causal connection with the satisfaction of this need;

3) Human knowledge of this causal connection; and
4) Command of the thing sufficient to direct it to the satisfaction of the
    need.

The four points stress the subjective and hermeneutical nature of goods. In
fact, if a thing does not respond to a *subjective* need, it cannot be classified as
a *good,* it simply remains a thing. Prerequisite 1, therefore, can be identified
with expectations. It should be followed by prerequisite 3, which can be seen
as the choice of the ends/means framework defined by expectations. From my
perspective, moreover, rerequisite 3 is a hermeneutical one: The possibility for
a thing to satisfy a need is not primarily an objective one; initially, the thing is
thought to be suitable for a need satisfaction. Human mind subjectively
interprets the object, imagining it able to meet the need under examination.
Only now prerequisite 2 can be taken into account: Things reveal their attitude
(characteristics) to satisfy needs through a discovery process, the result of the
testing procedure over the previous hermeneutical decision. Prerequisite 4 is
the implementation of a plan and cannot be separated from prerequisite 2.
Once expectations are formed and a certain ends/means framework is thought
to be consistent with them, the choice of the framework is tested through
implementation processes revealing, in time, the correctness of our
hermeneutical intuitions or the necessity for a revision. In order for a thing to
become a "good," therefore, it is necessary primarily to be thought as suitable
for a need satisfaction, and afterward such suitability needs to be tested in
reality. The initial hermeneutical process can find confirmation or denial:
Subjective processes need always to find confirmation in the factual reality. I
am free to think of a watch as suitable to cut a steak; but the practical test of
my hypothesis would frustrate my expectations. Subjective and objective sides
of reality complete each other.

It must be noted that this testing process is never at rest. In fact, a thing
could lose, or acquire, good status if circumstances change. The important
elements remain unchanged: expectations, interpreting some means as suitable
to achieve ends, testing the intuition through a plan implementation, and
revising plans as a consequence of information acquired during plan
implementation. Now, how to distinguish between goods and capital goods? I
believe that Mengerian distinction between higher- and lower-order goods is
not enough. Similarly, Lachmann's heterogeneous stock of material resources
does not help, it seems to be recursive: What are material resources, then?
Lachmann (1956, XV) added confusion in arguing that certain *goods* "are
capital not by virtue of their physical properties but by virtue of their

economic functions. Something is capital because the market, the consensus of entrepreneurial minds, regards it as capable of yielding an income." While I can agree with the first part of the statement, the second part, linking capital and income, sees Lachmann dangerously sliding onto a Böhm-Bawerkian or neo-Ricardian trap.

As mentioned, the Mengerian distinction between higher- and lower-order goods also seems to be inadequate. In fact, is it really possible to distinguish when a good is directly serving a need and when it is only participating in a process to get a lower order good? Look at a machine, for example. Common sense would judge it as at a capital good and Menger would be on the same page, imagining the machine to contribute to producing something that would satisfy more direct needs. But, at the same time, the very same machine is also serving a direct need, that is the entrepreneurial need to produce things. It could be argued that first-order goods are directly consumed and cannot be used a second time, while higher-order goods can serve their purposes several times—their consumption is spread over time. However, the possibility of a one-time use juxtaposed with a multiple-time usage seems not able to grasp the ontological essence of capital goods.

My distinction uses Menger as a starting point and tries to move beyond him. The basic distinction between consumption goods and capital goods is that the latter enter production processes. As we shall clarify later (paragraph 5), from this perspective labor must also be considered as a capital good. The second characteristics of capital goods, deriving from the first, is that they cannot serve their mission by themselves but only in combination with other capital goods. It is true, however, as pointed out by Lachmann, that such goods are *capital goods* by virtue of an economic function and not because of certain physical characteristics. It means that they need to be *thought* as suitable to enter a production process in combination with other goods, and generate a certain result. Our definition for *capital goods*, therefore, is as follows: *capital goods are goods that, in a specific moment in time, are* thought *to be suitable to generate a certain output when combined with other goods in a production process unfolding in time*. It will be the unfolding of the production process which will confirm their suitability as capital goods.

More specifically, we must then distinguish two categories of capital goods:

1) *Potential capital goods*: They are what we defined above, *stricto sensu*. Potential *capital goods* are *goods* that, in a specific moment in time, are thought to be suitable for generating a certain output when combined with other goods in a production process unfolding in time.

2) *Actual capital goods*: Goods that, in a specific moment in time, after being thought as suitable for generating a certain output when combined with other *goods* in a production process unfolding in time, are actually implemented in such a production process.

The *physical* definition of *capital* shall reflect the above distinction. Physically speaking, then, we might say that, in any given moment, potential capital is the set of potential capital goods, which means the set of goods that will be combined into production processes because they are thought, in a specific moment, to be suitable for implementing plans imagined to achieve ends dictated by expectations. Actual capital consists, on the other hand, of the set of goods that, in a specific moment, are actual capital goods, goods combined into productions processes in order to achieve desired ends. In both cases, capital is therefore not simply a set of goods. And, at the same time, it is not simply a set of productive combinations of goods. We are talking about a set of productive combinations of goods consciously implemented because they are *thought* to be the logical outcome of plans set in motion by the intention of fulfilling expectations.

It might seem that there is no difference between potential and actual capital. However, the first difference lies in the distinct moments in time at which the two entities come into being; potential capital refer to the moment at which the ends/means framework, following expectation formation, is generated into the economic actor mind (hermeneutical moment); actual capital, on the other hand, appears when plans thought to be consistent with the ends/means framework are implemented (operational/implementation moment). But potential and actual capital can be distinguished also for another reason: the hermeneutical moment could identify as capital goods some things which are not actually at the disposal of the individual for several reasons. Therefore, a second hermeneutical process would be needed, at a separate moment, in order to identify an alternative. The formation of the *actual capital* (implementation moment), thus, could happen, theoretically speaking, only after several hermeneutical moments take place.

It is now clear what I have in mind when I talk about *hermeneutics* of *capital*. The identification of capital goods is, first of all, a hermeneutical process in which active minds operate on objects after expectation formation has already happened. Capital without expectations cannot exist, therefore, precisely because capital is a characteristic attributed to objects by the subjective interpretation process operated by individuals who try to fulfill expectations. Plan implementation is the link between potential and actual capital.

Given such clarification, then, all the typical features of capital identified by Austrian economics apply to both our ideas of potential and actual capital. First of all, as we shall see in more detail below, capital is a heterogeneous set of goods, which acquire their capital characteristics only by virtue of being used together (combined) in a production process. To look to capital as a stock or as a sort of aggregate is impossible, and this gives rise to a lot of problems when we have to define capital in monetary terms (see paragraph 2.4).

The preferential position for observing capital, consequently, is not the abstract macroeconomic vision typical of neo-classics and Keynesians. The appropriate place, as pointed out by Lachmann (1976e, 310), is the company, if we mean it as the context in which subjective entrepreneurial interpretative processes happen (see Chapter 2).

One of the fundamental features of capital goods is that they are not perpetual: They are consumed in the course of a subsequent production process or become obsolete (Huerta de Soto 2000, 49; Rothbard 1962, 53). This means that after several implementation moments, capital goods can lose their attributes and therefore new hermeneutical processes are necessary in order to identify new capital formation paths.

Another characteristic of capital goods is that they become progressively more difficult to retransform the closer they come to the final stage of consumption (Huerta de Soto 2000, 49–50). This means that as we move closer to final consumption stages and alternative solutions are more difficult to imagine, hermeneutical processes of capital goods will become more complicated.

So far I only referred to capital from a micro perspective, which means referring to goods combined in order to achieve certain ends, without taking into account if and how it is possible to refer to capital at a macro level, considering the economic system as a whole. This is what I will try to do in paragraph 2.5.

2.4. Capital Value

It is now moment to try to understand if and how capital can be measured, that is, if it is possible to find a quantitative measure for capital and capital goods. As acknowledged in Lachamnn (1941) and Lewin (2011), in fact, the heterogeneous nature of capital goods create several problems in order to reach a meaningful measurement for the value of capital goods. Several options are also presented and analyzed by Kirzner (1966, 94–122).

Another question to be answered is whether capital measurement has a meaning at all. Why should we be interested in knowing the value of capital goods? In the end, what matters is the value of the output generated by capital goods intended as described above. An actual measure of capital can be interesting only to scholars conceiving rate of profit as the return rate on capital and therefore interpreting the profitability of investment as related to the employment of capital goods which can be aggregated and objectively measured. Instead, as suggested above and as will be clarified later, I look at profit as the difference between the price at which a good is sold and the sum of costs necessary to produce it. Profit, therefore, has a microeconomic nature, ignored by the aggregative approach.

However, some attempt of definition can be done. What cannot be measured is the value of single capital goods. Of course, individual capital goods have a market value, a price, intended as the objective synthesis of subjective evaluation processes. But to identify the value of a single capital good with its market value is meaningless, according to the definition of capital I brought out in this chapter. In fact, as we have seen, certain things acquire capital good status only in the moment in which they are thought to be suitable to achieve an end when combined with other goods into an intertemporal production process. What has meaning, thus, is the value of capital (potential or actual) intended as the productive combination of certain goods.

It now useful to recall our definition of capital (potential and actual). At any given moment, potential capital is the set of potential capital goods, which means the set of goods that will be combined into production processes because they are thought, in a specific moment, to be suitable to implement plans imagined to achieve ends dictated by expectations. Actual capital consists, on the other hands, of the set of goods that, in a specific moment, are actual capital goods, goods combined into productions processes in order to achieve desired ends. In both cases, capital is a set of productive combinations of goods consciously implemented because *thought* to be the logical outcome of plans set in motion by the intention of fulfilling expectations.

What we are looking for, thus, is the value of each productive combination at different moments in time. I believe that, for a certain output at the hermeneutical moment of time, the value of potential capital is the expected value (expected market price) of the desired output, discounted for the realization time (d) at an interest rate intended as the measure of the temporal preference (see below, paragraph 3). It is therefore clear that a measure of capital is completely subjective (Lewin 1996, 283).

Given:

PC = Potential Capital;

EO = Expected Output meant to be obtained with PC;

V_{EO} = Expected Value (market price) of EO at the realization moment (x);

T_n = Time at which PC is thought (hermeneutical moment, n);

T_x = Time at which EO is expected to be sold, where $x > n$;

$d = x$-n (distance between the realization moment x and the hermeneutical moment n);

i = interest rate (intertemporal preference measure) at time n;

V_{PC} = Value of PC at time n;

Then:

$$V_{PC} = V_{EO} - [(V_{EO} * i * d)/100] \tag{1}$$

Things become slightly more complicated when we want to define the value of actual capital, because of the different moment of time involved in the plan implementation process. For a certain output at any given moment in time, the value of actual capital is the expected value (expected market price) of the desired output, discounted for the realization time at an interest rate intended as the measure of the temporal preference. Therefore, the value of actual capital changes according to the different moments at which we are looking at it.

Given:

$AC_{n(1...x-\varepsilon)}$ = Actual Capital at different moments, where (x-ε) is the instant before EO is sold;

EO = Expected Output meant to be obtained with AC;

V_{EO} = Expected Value (market price) of EO at the realization moment (x);

$T_{n[1...(x-\varepsilon)]}$ = Time at which AC is observed (different implementation moments);

T_x = Time at which EO is expected to be sold, where $x>n$;

$d_{n(1...x-\varepsilon)}$ = $x-n_{(1...x-\varepsilon)}$ (distances between the realization moment and the different implementation moments);

$i_{n(1...x-\varepsilon)}$ = interest rates (intertemporal preference measure) at different implementation moments;

$V_{ACn(1...x-\varepsilon)}$ = Value of AC at different implementation moments; Then:

$$V_{ACn(1...x-\varepsilon)} = V_{EO} - [(V_{EO} * i_{n(1...x-\varepsilon)} * d_{n(1...x-\varepsilon)})/100] \qquad (2)$$

It is therefore clear that, regarding AC, we have to define its value according to the moment at which it is observed and evaluated. What makes the difference in the evaluation at different times is not only the discount period, which becomes gradually longer but also the interest rate, which, measuring the intertemporal preferences, presents an unpredictable path. Therefore we cannot conclude, as we move from n to x, that the value of the actual capital increases because of the unpredictability of the measure of the interest rate, which is subject to all the modifications that can happen in the flow of the real/historical time.

Actual capital can also be evaluated at the moment x, when the output is actually sold.

$$V_{ACx} = V_{EOx} - [(V_{EOx} * i_x * d)/100] \qquad (3)$$

This is a privileged moment of observation, for the realization value is actually known and not simply expected. Moreover, such evaluation keeps in account the temporal preference at the realization moment x. V_{ACx} can then be compared with V_{PC} assuming that the potential capital become actual capital (the thought goods are actually implemented into combinations). Then we can encounter the following scenarios.

Table 1. V_{ACx} and V_{PC} relationship according to according to` V_{EOx} and V_{Eon} and i_x and i_n relationships.

V_{EOx} and V_{EOn}	i_x and i_n	Result
$V_{EOx} = V_{EOn}$	$i_x = i_n$	$V_{ACx} = V_{PCn}$
$V_{EOx} > V_{EOn}$	$i_x = i_n$	$V_{ACx} > V_{PCn}$
$V_{EOx} < V_{EOn}$	$i_x = i_n$	$V_{ACx} < V_{PCn}$
$V_{EOx} > V_{EOn}$	$i_x > i_n$	$V_{ACx} > V_{PCn}$
$V_{EOx} < V_{EOn}$	$i_x > i_n$	$V_{ACx} < V_{PCn}$
$V_{EOx} > V_{EOn}$	$i_x < i_n$	$V_{ACx} > V_{PCn}$
$V_{EOx} < V_{EOn}$	$i_x < i_n$	$V_{Acx} < V_{PCn}$
$V_{EOx} = V_{EOn}$	$i_x > i_n$	$V_{Acx} < V_{PCn}$
$V_{EOx} = V_{EOn}$	$i_x < i_n$	$V_{Acx} > V_{PCn}$

Table 1 tells us that, if the interest rate at the realization moment and at the hermeneutical moments does not change, then the sign of the difference between V_{ACx} and V_{PCn} is given by the sign of the difference between V_{EOx} and V_{EOn}. When, on the other hand, the realization value is exactly the same as expected at the hermeneutical moment, then V_{ACx} will be higher than V_{PCn} if the interest rate decreased between n and x, while V_{ACx} will be lower than V_{PCn} if during the production process the interest rate increased. If both V_{EO} and i are higher at moment x when compared with moment n, then V_{ACx} will be also higher than V_{PCn}. Conversely, V_{ACx} will be lower than V_{PCn} when both V_{EO} and i are lower at moment x when compared with moment n. Instead, in case of opposite directions taken by V_{EO} and i between x and n, the relationship between V_{ACx} and V_{PCn} will follow the direction of the difference between V_{EOx} and V_{EOn}. In synthesis, Table 1 shows us how the value of the actual capital at the realization moment can differ from the value of the actual capital at the beginning of the plan implementation process (supposing that the potential capital becomes actual capital), according to the different movement that we can experience in the interest rate and in the difference between the realized value of the output and the expected value of it.

Finally, we can define the average value of the actual capital as the average between the different evaluations done at distinct moments in time, between x and n.

$$AV_{AC} = (\textstyle\sum_1^{x-\varepsilon} A C n)/d \tag{4}$$

Formula (4) does not gives us an *objective* measure of capital value, but simply an average value of the different evaluations done at distinct moments in time. Capital value exists only with reference at a specific moment in time and it is determined by the expected realization value, by the flow of time and by the temporal preference (via interest rate). (4) can only be interpreted as a synthetic expression, without any pretense of being the actual value of capital, which instead changes during the flow of time.

It is necessary to re-stress that, as capital in physical terms, I defined the value of capital *only* with reference to expectations and plans implemented in order to achieve the ends dictated by said expectations. It is only in such sense that we can talk meaningfully about capital goods and capital value. With reference to capital value in particular, it can be noted since I radically ignored any relation to the market value of the goods combined into production processes: The value of capital, intended as a combination, can be meaningfully interpreted only using the expected output as reference point. It is the output, as a human desire, which gives meaning to capital; therefore the value of the latter can be interpreted by active minds only with reference to the expected realization value of the former.

To summarize: Capital, in physical and monetary terms, exists only in relationship with some expected output. Such expected output allows us define and evaluate capital. Therefore, I never talked of capital in general terms, but always in connection with a specific ends/means framework, strictly related to individual expectations.

Also in measuring the value of capital, so far I have limited my analysis to the evaluation of single combinations and referred to the implementation of plans related to specific expectations. Again, I have confined my analysis at the micro level, without considering, as much as possible, capital as a whole with reference to the economic system. This element is what I will try to consider in the next section.

2.5. Capital Structure and the Production Process

After focusing in analyzing capital goods and capital value with exclusive reference to individual expectations, can we move from the micro to the macro level in the attempt to find a suitable definition for capital as referred to the economy as a whole? Some effort in this direction was done by Austrian economists.

As we have seen before, one of the most important elements in Austrian theory of capital lies in not referring to it as a macroeconomic aggregate. Instead, the Austrians, in resuming the Mengerian tradition, preferred a reference to various capital goods by acknowledging the heterogeneous nature (Lachmann, 1956, p. 2; Horwitz, 2000, p. 47) of a set of goods that cannot be constituted as an aggregate (Foss, 2012).

As is well known, to overcome such obstacles and to develop a structural perspective on capital, some Austrian economists built on the concept of production period or length of the production process (Hayek 1941, 70). In truth, as Hayek (1941, p. 70) admitted, it is difficult to think about the production period or the length of the production process in aggregate terms.[22] This is precisely because of the inhomogeneous nature of capital. Hayek (1931, 39) tried to overcome the difficulty introducing the so-called Hayek's *triangle*. The base of the right-angled triangle is the production period. The height measures the value of the final consumption goods produced during the production process. The various vertical distances between the hypotenuse and the axis of time are the values of the goods in production. Consequently, the hypotenuse is the value added by time and additional input. The intention is to illustrate the intertemporal structure of capital using certain basic concepts of Austrian theory, such as "production period' and ''roundabout' production. However, it seems that such an instrument does not render justice to capital as I have defined it.

Before trying to define capital for an economic system, and following the traditional Austrian approach, I will refer to the *capital structure*. First of all we can define the *potential capital structure* as the set of all the combinations that are, at a specific moment, thought to be suitable to fulfill expectations when implemented into production processes. Similarly, the *actual capital structure* is the set of all the combinations of actual capital goods which are implemented, following plans designed to fulfill expectations. Such definitions directly derive from the previous ones but probably fail to deepen the understanding of the shape taken by the structure itself.

This structure, which is determined by expectations and production plans, can hardly be viewed as stable over time. It is therefore evident that the neoclassical function of production, in which there is no process but simply the relationship between output and the combination of capital and labor, is unable to grasp the essence of the production process as the combination, over time, of capital goods.

---

[22] Rothbard (1962, 52): "Again, it must be observed that, in considering the length of a process of production, the actor is not interested in past history as such. The length of a process of production for an actor is the waiting-time from the point at which his action begins."

> [T]he neoclassical constant-returns production function [...] does not describe production as a process, i.e., as an ordered sequence of operations. It is more like a recipe for bouillabaisse where all the ingredients are dumped in a pot, (K, L), heated up, f(*), and the output, X, is ready. This abstraction from the sequencing of tasks, it will be suggested, is largely responsible for the well-known fact that neoclassical production theory gives us no clue to how production is actually organized. (Leijonhufvud 1986, 203–204).

Even if, in order to bring out the desired output, certain goods combinations need to be implemented for a prolonged amount of time, we cannot look at the capital structure as something stable. The amount of goods combinations implemented over time is so high that something is always changing somewhere. Moreover, the various combinations are interlinked since they are complementary or replaceable. There are also combinations that become unsuitable, and therefore such goods can no longer be considered as capital.

> The capital structure of society is an aggregate of capital combinations, but only in a state of general equilibrium can the capital goods belonging to different firms be regarded as additive, when the stand to each other in a relationship of *complementarity*. It is, however, a type of complementarity different from that governing capital goods within the same capital combination. We have to distinguish between the planned complementarity of the latter, the result of entrepreneurial choice and decision, and the unplanned complementarity of capital resources at various stages of production, which is an outcome of the operation of the market process. (Lachmann 1976e, 311, my italics).

The form that the structure of capital takes is thereby defined by none other than production plans, which use different combinations of capital goods. The relative extents to which these factors become part of the combinations (production coefficients) identify the extent to which these factors are complementary to each other (Lachmann 1947, 204).

> [T]he proportions in which the various capital resources enter [a combination] express the mode of capital complementarity in it, what we shall call the *capital coefficients*. The capital coefficients in each combination are thus the ultimate determinants of the capital structure, at

least in equilibrium. In disequilibrium the degree of consistency between plans is a modifying factor. (Lachmann 1947, 204).

However, as hinted by Lachmann (1976e, 312) himself, the real world is constantly in disequilibrium, and therefore entrepreneurs will have to continually seek new ways to group capital goods together in order to adapt to the changes taking place.

A certain capital structure, as defined above (potential or actual), can be observed only in a well-defined instant. The kaleidoscope metaphor used by Lachmann and Shackle is appropriate: In the very moment at which our eyes are grasping the shape of such a structure, it is already changing, or, better, it is evolving in order to adapt itself to the evolution of the hermeneutical process of expectation formation. We may say that, at any moment, capital goods are combined into processes in order to achieve results: capital structure exists but has no shape. Or, better, at any moment it reshapes in order to adapt itself to mind processes never at rest. The *blob* is probably the best image we can have in mind when thinking about capital structure: contractions and expansion continuously happen in all directions.

Is there any space in such analysis for traditional Austrian concepts like *roundaboutness* and *length of the production process*? In fact, they are central elements for other crucial themes of Austrian economics, particularly for business cycle theory. Certainly reality shows moments when this becomes more evident as a relatively high number of capital combinations are devoted toward the production of a specific good able to give birth to high profit expectations. Such phenomena usually, but not necessarily, imply longer production times and can be identified with innovations or speculations (often related). I will consider the emergence of these specific kinds of capital combinations in chapter 3.

3. INTEREST AND PROFIT

3.1. Neo-Austrians beyond Böhm-Bawerk: Intertemporal Preferences and Interest Rate

Lachmann's criticism of Böhm-Bawerk is only the initial point of a general attempt, inside the Austrian school, to build a new capital theory able to go beyond the neo-Ricardian formalism, without, at the same time, wasting the positive insights contained inside the traditional version of the Austrian

Capital Theory. Such attempts brought out the so-called *pure-time preference theory of interest*, which I consider consistent with my approach to capital theory.

The first attempts to redirect the ACT along Mengerian lines was done by Frank Fetter and Ludwig von Mises, with the development of the pure-time preference theory of interest (PTPT), in which the vision of time as ingredient (which leaves the door open to productivistic views on interest) is rejected in favor of an approach based on time as the general container for economic processes. As explained by Lewin (2011, 111–112),

> [...] interest does not depend in any way on the productivity of capital. [...] The *rental return* to capital is conceptually quite distinct from interest. Interest is not the return on capital. [...] A positive time preference is a necessary and sufficient condition for the existence of interest. [...] Interest is thus "explained" by the propensity of individuals to discount the future.

In order to define the PTPT properly, it is necessary to embrace the concept of time I described at the beginning of the present chapter. The definition of time developed by post-Böhm-Bawerk Austrians marks an intergenerational change inside the school. As described above, O'Driscoll and Rizzo (1985) distinguished real time from Newtonian time and linked the first one to the inevitable ignorance that characterizes the process of human action. While Böhm-Bawerk elaborated on his theory to include a logical time framework (which allowed him to unfold the concepts of time preference and interest), from Hayek onward Austrians shifted into the historical time ground, which is a vehicle of novelty and source of uncertainty.

It is only a concept of time such as this that allows Austrians to include in the schema two other fundamental elements: time preferences and the inter-temporal structure of production. Thanks to the combination of such factors, a completely different definition of interest rate arises.

According to the law of time preference, other things being equal, humans always place present goods higher than future goods on their scale of values; on this assumption, we can define the interest rate as the market price of present goods in terms of future goods. Neo-Austrians, then, depart from the traditional vision of interest rates as the cost of money or marginal productivity of capital. Such a vision, at the root of the pure temporal preference theory of interest, can arise only in the context of historical time, because time preference is not conceivable outside a world of uncertainty.

Therefore, neo-Austrians define an interest rate for the economic system that measures the more general structure of time preferences. In a future-oriented system, consumers are more savings-oriented, thereby encouraging the accumulation of loanable funds that can be used by entrepreneurs in long-term projects. A present-oriented society, in contrast, has a greater propensity toward consumption on the consumer side, while investors do not lengthen the production process. The level of equilibrium for a combination of time preferences and measured by the so-called natural interest rate corresponds to a defined structure of the production process. Intertemporal preferences, therefore, via the interest rate, determine the pace of capital investment and the extent of capital accumulation. As anticipated by Mises, and developed by Hayek, it is necessary to sacrifice the production of consumer goods in order to divert resource for investment projects (via saving).

Time preference can be described simply by arguing that the value of a certain object, or a certain amount of money, today is not the same as the value of that object of amount of money two years from now. As Rothbard (1987, 59) clearly stated, time preference:

> [. . .] is the insight that people prefer "present goods" (goods available for use at present) to "future goods" (present expectations of goods becoming available at some date in the future), and that the social rate of time preference, the result of the interactions of individual time-preference schedules, will determine and be equal to the pure rate of interest in a society.

Therefore the interest rate finds its own justification only in the passage of time. As explained by Lewin (2011, 115), "[c]omparing the purchase of (a) a prospect that is ranked 1 today with (b) a prospect that would be ranked 1 today if it were available today but is only available tomorrow; since (as indicated by the ranking) (a) is preferred to (b), time preference exists."

It is implicit in such a definition that time preference exists because the flow of time implies *uncertainty*. Therefore, the interest rate cannot be seen as the yield gained on the usage of some capital goods (Mises 2011, 67). On the contrary, uncertainty ontological to the flow of historical time generates a natural tendency in human beings to prefer present goods to future goods. The intensity of such preference, called *time preference*, constitutes the natural interest rate.

Such a concept of interest rate, even if not measuring the return on capital, is closely related to hermeneutical processes of capital formation, centered on the concept of human action. Human action is the process of plan implementation set in motion in order to define the ends/means framework, which in turn is defined consistently with expectations. However, as the implementation of plans is a process which unfolds over (historical/real) time, expectations revision drives toward a continuous change in the ends/means framework and therefore in the implemented plans. Expectations are defined consistently with time preferences, which are the key element in the definition of production processes consistent with such preferences. A shift in time preferences can drive toward capital destruction, capital creation, or, in general, capital re-shaping; the central signal guiding these processes of capital formation is given by the interest rate intended as the synthesis measure of the intertemporal structure of preferences, mirrored by a defined intertemporal structure of production. Interest rate is no more linked with a necessary measurement of capital. On the contrary, variations in the interest rate (as a measure of the intertemporal structure of preferences) potentially generate a modification in the intertemporal structure of production and therefore in the structural composition of capital and not the reverse. A capital, in turn, that can be viewed only in its ever-changing, intertemporal, structural composition, avoids any possibility of being defined as an aggregate (social or individual).

3.2. Entrepreneurial Profit

As in the previous section where I completely disconnected the interest rate from the concept of return on capital, a similar process needs to be done in defining *profit*. As it should be clear from our discussion so far, it is only in the realm of expectational (historical) time that profit can be generated (Shackle 1972, chapter 35). In fact, historical time, as the framework into which novelty and uncertainty are generated, allows profit opportunities to appear and to be exploited by entrepreneurial alertness. If there were no uncertainty, "there would be no profit. All production plans in such a world would be successful" (Lewin 2011, 117). While in a context of logical time the concept of *waiting* is a sufficient element in bringing out Böhm-Bawerk's idea of interest intended as ''marginal productivity of waiting' (Wicksell 1893, 21-22), only the *uncertainty* ontological to the concept of historical time can bring out profit as necessary outcome of a context of limited knowledge (about the present conditions of other actors and about the future status of the economic system).

Ignoring the microfoundations of macroaggregates, Ricardo, Marx, neo-Ricardians, Keynes, and even Böhm-Bawerk, according to Lachmann, assumed capital to be homogeneous; this allowed them to define unequivocally a uniform rate of profit linked with the return on capital.[23] Therefore, while Böhm-Bawerk and Hayek (i.e., 1941, 354) remained connected with the classics in linking capital and the rate of profit, successive generations of Austrians parted this view, associating profit with entrepreneurial activity. Lachmann (1973a, 26) argued that, first of all, profit needs to be considered simply as the difference between the price at which a commodity is sold and its cost to the seller. As we will see in Chapter 2, to find a way to sell goods at prices above the production costs is the essence of entrepreneurial activity; as such, profit can sprout only from a disequilibrium situation, because in equilibrium all profit opportunities are already exploited.

The vision of profit as the result of entrepreneurial activity is at best described by Kirzner (1973, 48). Also Schumpeter (1934, 128) simply defined *profit* as a surplus over costs, a difference between receipts and outlay generated by entrepreneurial action, adding (1928, 66–271) that interest on capital is a remuneration that has to be kept out from profit *stricto sensu*.

Profit, therefore, does not have anything to do with the supposed productivity of capital. In fact, such productivity could be defined only if it would be possible to define *capital* as an aggregate. At the same time, all the classic and neo-classic discussions about the rate of return lose their meaning; in fact, as to the concept of productivity, they are strictly concerned with the possibility of reaching an aggregate definition of *capital*. As explained in Lewin (1996, 280), for these economists the "rate of profit [. . .] is a flow of incomes received by the owners of wealth divided by the stock of capital. Hence with the rate of profit being the prime focus of interest, the size of the capital stock had to be considered by implication."

As we have seen, instead, we can only define the value of capital in a specific moment and as related to specific combinations implemented to obtain an output. According to my vision, moreover, capital value is changing with the flow of time, being determined by the expected value of the output, by the interest rate, and by time itself. Profit, therefore, can be analyzed only from a micro perspective, as the result of entrepreneurial activity.

With the neo-Austrian definition (linking profit to entrepreneurial activity), which I share, profit can have also a negative magnitude. In the

---

[23] To define the concept of uniform rate of profit (intended as the situation in which return on various capital investments are equal), Ricardo initiated a tradition of refering to a situation of long-run equilibrium as a *constant state of affairs*.

market economy, each company or entrepreneur acts in order to maximize profit; however, *motivation* toward a positive profit and *success* in achieving the target are different things. The very nature of the market economy renders the success of all plans impossible (Lachmann 1973a, 26). Equilibrium exists only *ex ante*: plans are consistent with expectations and the limited available content of information. But, *ex post*, it is possible to discover that one plan was inadequate to reach the target. Malinvestment can actually happen. Therefore, there is "no such thing […] as *a rate* of profit, there are only *rates* of profit which may differ widely" (Lachmann 1973a, 26). Each rate of profit is related, as capital, to a specific output and the specific combination of goods implemented in order to obtain it. Therefore, it is not possible to define a rate of profit for the economic system. Instead, we can define profit and rate of profit for each specific output, starting from the actual capital used in the production process. Remember formula (3):

$$V_{ACx} = V_{EOx} - [(V_{EOx} * i_x * d)/100] \tag{3}$$

Profit for a certain output (P_{EOx}) would be thus defined:

$$P_{EOx} = V_{EOx} - \Sigma C_{EOx} \tag{5}$$

Where ΣC_{EOx} is the sum of all the costs encountered in order to get EO_x. The rate of profit for the same output (RP_{EOx}) will be:

$$RP_{EOx} = (P_{EOx}/V_{EOx})*100 \tag{6}$$

Ricardians could not accept the fact that we cannot define a rate of profit for the whole economic system because of the micro nature of entrepreneurial action and the heterogeneity of capital. Even two identical machines can bring out different results if used in different ways or under different conditions of time and space. Profit is not simply related to the physical features of capital but above all to capital *combinations*: capital can produce a profit if used in *a certain* way (Lachmann 1956, 3–12): entrepreneurial function needs to be at work in continuously rearranging the capital structure (Lachmann 1956, 13). This makes it impossible to talk about a *uniform rate of profit* (Lachmann 1973a, 27) or *marginal productivity of capital*.

As mentioned earlier, following Shackle and his accent on expectational time as the context for uncertainty to generate profit, Lachmann (1973a, 31) and the neo-Austrians in general define *profit* as *essentially* and *ontologically* a disequilibrium phenomenon. Being generated by the difference between selling prices and purchasing costs, profits cannot arise in an equilibrium context. In the struggle for profit, entrepreneurial function will wake up equilibrating forces, but profit will be present to the extent that such equilibrium does not prevail; and in a kaleidic world (historical time) this is the case: Coordination tendencies are at work but they never prevail as the equilibrium itself is continuously changing.

Entrepreneurial function, seeking for profits, moves the market from a disequilibrium status on a coordination path toward equilibrium (Kirzner 1973, 69–75). The starting point of human action, in fact, is always a state of disequilibrium, characterized by market ignorance. It is through interaction in the market that knowledge can be transmitted and acquired, bringing out plan revisions. Entrepreneurial alertness allows such changes to happen and, therefore, by reducing market ignorance and driving plans toward mutual compatibility, it is an *equilibrating* force. The equilibrating process consists exactly in the acquisition of better mutual information concerning the plans made by the different market actors (Kirzner 1963, 38). It is only in disequilibrium that profit opportunities actually exist and can be discovered by entrepreneurial alertness (Kirzner 1992, 5). In this sense, alertness allows discovery, and discovery plays an equilibrating role, reducing market ignorance. However, in opposition to Kirzner, Lachmann stated that such equilibrating forces, in the market economy, cannot prevail, and this fact gives meaning to the competitive process: Profit persists in the market because disequilibrium is always present in some sector of economic system (Lachmann 1973a, 32).

Lachmann (1973a, 32) drew two conclusions from his analysis on the nature of profit:

> First, the ever-elusive and fugitive price-cost differences which are the source of all profits can have no place in the long-term equilibrium world to which the two rival schools [Cambridge and neo-classical schools] are both committed. *An equilibrium rate of profit is thus a contradiction in terms.*
>
> Secondly, profits are pre-eminently a micro-economic phenomenon. Their basis is to be found primarily in the ever-changing pattern of price-cost differences in a thousand different markets. Without understanding this micro-foundation of the phenomenon we cannot understand its essence. We certainly should not be able to formulate a general theory of

profits without it. A macro-economic theory of profit can therefore make little sense.

According to Lachmann (1973a, 33–35), from the Ricardian perspective which is implicit in Böhm-Bawerk's capital theory, we miss the opportunity to understand the true nature of profit, lying in the micro forces of the market competition process. We can say that Böhm-Bawerk, in his analysis of profit and capital, started to develop new ideas but remained linked with the aggregative approach of the classical economists, an approach from which neo-Austrians parted completely, developing a micro perspective of profit as the result of entrepreneurial action. When we talk about wealth and capital, we might say that Böhm-Bawerk, like Marx, developed, although in different directions, Smith's hints.

Post-Böhm-Bawerk Austrians followed a complete different path and clearly identified profit as the result of entrepreneurial activity. We should then talk about profit generated by different economic initiatives, a magnitude that can be negative. The time dimension, producing endless changes in the economic scenario, can be considered as the key to understanding the perpetual nature of profit, according to the neo-Austrians. Time changes information content and therefore the tendency toward equilibrium operate in a context in which such equilibrium is always changing. The kaleidoscopic nature of economic activity makes profit opportunities always present to be discovered by entrepreneurial alertness.

In conclusion, neo-Austrians, through an analysis developed in the historical time framework, stress the importance of entrepreneurial action *in time* as perpetual source of profit. This perspective, however, skipped past Böhm-Bawerk's focus on the justification of interest rate in the context of logical time.

4. A WRONG WORD: *CAPITALISM*

I close this chapter with a terminological digression. In fact, due to cultural reasons, influences, and evolutions, *capitalism* has become a word full of ideological contents. Defenders of free market economy use it to describe the phantasmagoric evolution of the world economy after the industrial revolution. Leftists, on the other hand, summarize with that word all the possible negative implications of the relationship between employers and employees (conflict between capital and labor), together with supposed injustices brought out by economic development and globalization processes. Historically speaking, instead, the term is often used to describe an economic evolution process beginning in the Mediterranean basin after the Crusades.

Braudel (1979, 232–239) investigated the origin of the word itself. If the world *capital* can already be found in the Italian economic life of the thirteenth century (232–233), the word *capitalist* "probably dates from the mid-seventeenth century. The *Hollandische Mercurius* uses it once in 1633, and again in 1654. In 1699, a French memorandum notes that a new tax [. .] distinguishes between "capitalists,who will pay 3 florins, and other people who will pay 30 sols"" (234–235). The origins and the meaning of the term *capitalism,* in contrast, appear to be more controversial. It can be found in the *Encyclopédie* in 1753, but with the exclusive purpose of identifying someone rich (237); in 1850, Louis Blanc instead defined *capitalism* as "the appropriation of capital by some to the exclusion of others" (237). Marx, to whom the word is often linked, never used it, talking only about a capitalistic mode of production.

Capitalism as a word entered the economic debate, in contrast to *socialism*, only at the beginning of the twentieth century, thanks to *Der modern Kapitalismus* by Werner Sombart, published in 1902 (Braudel 1979, 237). Since then the word was enriched by political meanings: If Marx never used it, Marxist economists use the terms "*slavery, feudalism* and *capitalism* [. . .] to refer to the three major stages of development defined by the author of *Capital*" (237).

Schumpeter (1942) described very well how the set of values usually contained into the word *capitalism* is undermined at its very root by a growing hostility emerging not from socialist or Marxist environments; rather, such hostility is a fruit growing in the capitalistic womb. Due to cultural evolution and the political usage of the word which began at the dawn of the twentieth century, "capitalism stands its trial before judges who have the sentence of death in their pockets" (Schumpeter 1942, 144). For such reasons, following Herbert Heaton and Lucien Febvre, Braudel (1979, 238), we suggest that such a word should be dropped.

In fact, the confusion and the ideological biases associated with this word make it more useless than useful, generating neverending debates about the good or evil nature of capitalism. Literally speaking, *capitalism* should refer to the use of capital in the production processes; in this way, the term would not be linked necessarily and solely with free market economies or private property. It goes without saying that also planned economies need capital goods in order to implement production processes.

The second source of confusion is to use the word *capitalism* in order to mark the contrast between capital and labor, as two distinct and often conflicting factors of production. Such a distinction penetrated economic theory so deeply that it is widely accepted as describing the "capitalistic mode of production" through the so-called aggregate production function (Solow 1956, 66; 1957, 312):

$$q = F(K,L)^{24}$$

(7)

Formula (7) is probably one of the most famous formulas studied in microeconomics and all students are familiar with it. Of course, it is true that a certain output is generated by the combination of capital goods as described above, and human intervention, which here is generally labelled as L. Apart from considerations regarding the measurability of K and L, and recalling our definition of actual capital, we have simply to conclude that L is not opposed or even complementary to K; quite the contrary: L is *included* in K. When we defined *actual capital* as the set of goods that are implemented together in production processes in real time in order to generate an output dictated by expectations, we naturally included labor in the goods which can be chosen to enter the capital combination. It must therefore be clear that labor has to be organically intended as a part of both the potential and the actual capital. In this way, the labor category has to be considered widely; *labor* includes tasks performed by workers in a factory, administrative roles covered by white collar workers, and also organizational and directional duties accomplished by managers and directors. Formula (7) can be rewritten as follows:

$$O_x = F(O_n;AC;tf)$$

(8)

Where O_x is the output at the end of the production process, O_n is the desired output (thought at the hermeneutical/expectational moment x), AC is the actual capital and tf is the time flow. This means that the output is not simply a function of labor and capital, but, more generally, is a function of expectations (O_n), of the actual capital (including different human functions usually labelled as labor) and of the time flow. It must be taken into account, moreover, that the shape of AC, between x and n, is not necessarily stable; it will have to readapt according to the novelty brought in by the implementation of the plan over time. It has to be added that, in defining O_x as function of O_n

---

[24] Pindyck and Rubinfeld (2013, 204).

(expectations), I do not intend this in a deterministic way; expectations do not univocally define the actual output, but of course they play the major role in defining the capital formation thought to be suitable for fulling them, and therefore they must be considered a nondeterministic determinant of the final outcome.

Because of the artificial juxtaposition between capital and labor, therefore, I suggest dropping the word *capitalism*, so that labor can be understood as an integral part of capital; this will not happen if the use of the expression *human capital* is constantly growing. The economic world is realizing that the human contribution to the production process is not simply a cost to be evaluated as an alternative to applying different production factors. On the contrary, human action enters directly the production process, and, when seen, in combination with other goods, to be suitable to fulfill expectations, becomes a capital good.

If the word *capitalism* would be abandoned, then, we would find ourselves without an expression to be used in juxtaposition to *socialism* or *planned economy*. However, sound alternatives are available. I suggest that *private property system* and *free market/competition* are expressions that could be used for the purpose without getting lost in ideological conversations. In fact, in talking about *private property* and *free market* we clearly state what we have in mind with regards to the legal framework in which economic actions take place. In contrast, the word *capitalism* cannot univocally identify the basic features of the economic system under consideration.

Chapter 2

CAPITAL AND ENTREPRENEURSHIP

1. INTRODUCTION

The aim of the present chapter is to develop a theory of entrepreneurship consistent with the capital theory explained in Chapter 1. In particular, it will be my task to define the relationships between entrepreneurial activity and capital formation. As Kirzner developed a middle ground between Lachmannian hermeneutics and Rothbard's praxeology, I will define my entrepreneurship theory looking for a middle ground between Schumpeter and Kirzner himself, expanding some hints presented in Ferlito (2015a).

Joseph A. Schumpeter developed a very well–known theory of entrepreneurs and entrepreneurship, centred on the concept of ''new combinations,'' introduced by special human types, entrepreneurs, conceived as *leaders* in the process of change. According to him, innovation and entrepreneurship are destructive elements driving the system beyond an equilibrium position and setting in motion a competitive process, in order to reach a new equilibrium point. Though Austrian, Schumpeter was never a member of the Austrian School of Economics. However, his position about entrepreneurship is widely commented on by Austrian School members. In particular, Israel M. Kirzner devoted his research activity to developing an alternative concept of entrepreneurship rooted in the Misesian human action and in the concept of "alertness" to previously unnoticed profit opportunities.

2. SCHUMPETER: THE ENTREPRENEUR AS A LEADER

Schumpeter's theory of innovation and entrepreneurship is so famous that it becomes necessary to briefly resummarize its main points, trying to follow Schumpeter's footsteps directly and, at the same time, to free his perspective from certain *clichés*. I will focus on the Schumpeterian entrepreneur as described in the first English translation of *Theorie* (1934), which refers to the second German edition (1926).[1].

First of all, it should be noted that Schumpeter's entrepreneurship vision must be analyzed as part of a more global perspective on the process of economic development. In developing his theory, Schumpeter described the entrepreneurial character only after having detailed what *development* means, its differences compared to the circular flow (and the place for static theory), the emergence of innovations and the role of bankers. The entire first part of Chapter 2 in Schumpeter (1934) is devoted to describing what economic development is and why it cannot be understood with the instruments of circular flow analysis.

> Development in our sense is a distinct phenomenon, entirely foreign to what may be observed in the circular flow or in the tendency towards equilibrium. It is spontaneous and discontinuous change in the channels of the flow, disturbance of equilibrium, which forever alters and displaces the equilibrium state previously existing. (Schumpeter 1934, 64).

Such changes, moreover, "are not forced upon [economic life] from without but arise by its own initiative, from within" (Schumpeter 1934, 63). Thus, the first important point is that economic development is a movement out from an existing equilibrium condition, a disturbance of such an equilibrium state. After this clarification, introducing the concept of "new combinations," Schumpeter described how economic development actually manifests itself.

> (1) The introduction of new goods—i.e., something with which consumers are not yet familiar—or a new quality of goods.
> (2) The introduction of a new method of production, that is one not yet tested by experience in the branch of manufacture concerned, which

---

[1] Thanks to Becker, Knudsen, and Swedberg (2011b), an English translation of the central chapters of the 1911 edition of *Theorie* is now available.

by no means has to be founded on a new, scientific discovery and can also exist as a new way of handling a commodity commercially.

(3) The opening of a new market, that is a market into which the particular branch of manufacture into which the country in question has not previously entered, whether or not this market had existed before.

(4) The conquest of a new source of supply of raw materials or semi-finished goods, again irrespective of whether this source already exists or whether it has first to be created.

(5) The carrying out of the new organization of any industry, such as the creation of a monopoly position (for example through trustification) or the breaking up of a monopoly position. (Schumpeter 1934, 66).

New combinations are, therefore, the essence of economic development. The second essential element of the economic development process is *credit*. Developing this point in Schumpeter (1934), the author marked an important difference with the Austrian economics tradition, led at that time by Ludwig von Mises. According to Schumpeter (1934, 69), "the possessor of wealth, even if it is the greatest combine, must resort to credit if he wishes to carry out a new combination, which cannot like an established business be financed by returns from previous production." This means that in no way new combinations can be brought out using existing saving. Therefore, there cannot be any economic development without the creation of debt; the Austrian School of Economics, in the same period, developed a business cycle theory arguing that sustainable development is possible only if investments are financed by existing savings. On the contrary, Schumpeter, although admitting that such a development process generates a boom and bust cycle, considered development impossible without what he called the "creation of purchasing power by banks" (Schumpeter 1934, 73). This is one of the strongest statements among Schumpeterian intuitions: the role of entrepreneurs is meaningless without the banker, who is, therefore, at least as important as the entrepreneur in carrying out new combinations, constituting the essence of the development process. Schumpeter (1934, 74) was very clear about it:

The banker, therefore, is not so much primarily a middleman in the commodity "purchasing power" as a *producer* of this commodity. [...] He makes possible the carrying out of new combinations, authorises people, in the name of society as it were, to form them. He is the ephor of the exchange economy.

However, new combinations and credit are not enough for the emergence of economic development. A further element is necessary, the one that Schumpeter (1934, 74) called the "fundamental phenomenon of economic development." In fact, if the carrying out of new combinations can be called "enterprise," "the individuals whose function it is to carry them out [are called] "entrepreneurs" (Schumpeter 1934, 74). It is at this point that Schumpeter started to develop his famous entrepreneur theory. It is therefore clear that "entrepreneur" and ''capitalists" are, functionally speaking, very distinct subjects, the former carrying out new combinations, the latter providing (creating) the purchasing power necessary for it.

But the central question is why "is the carrying out of new combinations a special process and the object of a special kind of "function" (Schumpeter 1934, 79), the entrepreneurial function? According to Schumpeter, in the realm of circular flow economic subjects are able to promptly and rationally act and react to given circumstances that repeat themselves over time. *Normal* individuals can face such an environment. But, when changes and innovations happen, normal individuals need *guidance* (Schumpeter 1934, 79). Because of the need for such guidance, "the carrying out of new combinations is a special function, and the privilege of a type of people who are much less numerous than all those who have the 'objective' possibility of doing it" (Schumpeter 1934, 81). Entrepreneurs are the special type of persons, with a special behavior, able to exercise such a guidance.

This is another crucial aspects that can be misunderstood, but about which Schumpeter (1934, 84–91) talked at length: *leadership*. Calling *innovation* the introduction of new combinations, Schumpeterian entrepreneur is rightly identified as *innovator*. The word is not free from ambiguity and misunderstandings. Though scholars often clarified that innovation is not necessarily a new invention, the risk to identify the entrepreneurial function with the invention of something new is high. However, the entrepreneur is not the inventor (Schumpeter 1947, 152). The entrepreneur is a special type not simply because he carries out new combinations but also because he, in doing so, masters a development process that is a process of change. Entrepreneurs, introducing new combinations into the economic system, demonstrate to be able to move where normal individuals stop.

According to Schumpeter (1934, 84–87), to move outside the boundaries of the circular flow is difficult for three kinds of reasons:

> First, outside these accustomed channels the individual is without
> those data for his decisions and those rules of conduct which are usually

very accurately known to him within them. Of course, he must still foresee and estimate on the basis of his experience. But many things must remain uncertain, still others are only ascertainable within wide limits, some can perhaps only be "guessed." [...]

Here the success of everything depends upon intuition. [...]

As this first point lies in the task, so the second lies in the psyche of the businessman himself. It is not only objectively more difficult to do something new than what is familiar and tested by experience, but he individual feels reluctance to it and would do so even if the objective difficulties did not exist. [...]

The third point consists in the reaction of the social environment against one who wishes to do something new. [...]

There is leadership *only* for these reasons.

These features need to be further stressed. Innovation is a change in the economic system (Schumpeter 1935, 4). Entrepreneur, introducing innovations, is a special human type because such changes cannot be faced and managed by normal individuals. In carrying out new combinations, entrepreneurs move the system outside the equilibrium state; but, moreover, after innovations are introduced, businessmen face the straggle of making the innovation win against "the old way" of doing things, against social hostility. In this struggle it is not the invention that characterizes the entrepreneur but his *leadership*, his ability to master the new situation. This is the reason why Schumpeter (1934, 88) stressed that it "is not part of his [entrepreneur's] function to "find" or to "create" new possibilities. They are always present, abundantly accumulated by all sorts of people."

While many people see things, the leader *does* things. It is therefore "more by will than by intellect that the leaders fulfill their function, more by "authority," "personal weight," and so forth than by original ideas" (Schumpeter 1934, 88). And economic leadership must be distinguished from invention. The emphasis on this aspect was even stronger in the first edition of *Theorie*:

You can always have the new combinations, but it is the act and the force to act that is indispensable and decisive. [...] The decisive moment is therefore energy and not merely the 'insight.' The latter is much more frequent, without leading to even the most simple act. What matters is the disposition to act. It is the *ability to subjugate others* and to utilize them for this purposes, in order to prevail that leads to successful deeds—even without particularly brilliant intelligence. (Schumpeter 1911, 123, italic added).

This is another element that we must bear in mind for our comparison with Kirzner's perspective: Leadership is a special attitude and therefore leaders are a special kind. This, as we shall see, sharply contrasts with the Kirznerian alertness as a basic feature of human action. Moreover, the emphasis on the *special character* belonging to entrepreneurs is one of the elements that Schumpeter did not change while evolving his vision of entrepreneurship.

The remuneration that makes its way into entrepreneur's pocket is called *profit*, that Schumpeter (1934, 128) simply defined as a surplus over costs, a difference between receipts and outlay. But with the word "outlay" Schumpeter meant all the disbursements which the entrepreneur has to make, including the salary for his own work, the price of the factors of production and the premium for risk. Therefore, profit is not the reward for the entrepreneur's labor, and it is not related to risk. Schumpeter (1928, 266–271) more analytically explained that there are several types of income that entrepreneurs can get, but that, at the same time, do not fall into the profit category: interest on capital, a salary for administrative work, revenues on patent rights, a premium for risk, "opportunistic profits" arising from seasonal factors. Entrepreneurial profits, instead, are linked with the entrepreneurial function, that is to bring out new combinations (Schumpeter 1928, 270–271). Because of such a link between entrepreneurial profit and entrepreneurial function, profit is, by nature, temporary (Schumpeter 1934, 132). In fact, under the impulse of profit, "new businesses are continually arising" (Schumpeter 1934, 131). Profit expectations, therefore, drive competitors and imitators to enter the world of new combinations; a complete reorganization of the affected industry happens, squeezing profits until they disappear and a new equilibrium state is reached. However, though temporary, profit exists, and it sprouts out from the very nature of the entrepreneurial function, the will and the action necessary to carry out new combinations (Schumpeter 1934, 132).

It is very well known that Schumpeter's vision of entrepreneurship evolved through the decades. The emphasis on the entrepreneur and his exceptional character, grounded on will and leadership, gave way to a deeper analysis of the entrepreneurial function (1926), while the carrying out of new combinations gradually lost its link with the entrepreneur *as a person*. Living the passage from the "heroic" stage of industrial development hallmarked by individual entrepreneurs to the next one characterized by the emergence of trusts, in Schumpeter (1939) new combinations called *innovations* were still present, and innovations became central to the business cycle analysis. Entrepreneurs are still there, but Schumpeter gradually recognized the declining importance of the entrepreneurial function in the age of trusts. Schumpeter did not renounce his view of entrepreneurs; he simply observed that the general economic scenario was changing:

> Already, the volitional aptitudes that made the successful entrepreneur of old are much less necessary and have much less scope than they used to have. It is no chance coincidence that the epoch in which this decrease in importance of the entrepreneurial function first asserted itself is also the epoch in which the social and political position of the *bourgeoisie* fist began to display obvious symptoms of weakness and to be attacked with success. (Schumpeter 1939, 109).

Such an observation is a bridge toward what in Schumpeter (1942, 131–134) was called the *obsolescence of the entrepreneurial function.* Schumpeter (1942, 132) observed that the peculiar function of "getting things done," the personal will, is losing importance because of two orders of reasons. On one hand, the task of innovation is becoming the activity of trained specialists. On the other hand, the social environment is becoming accustomed to economic change and therefore the resistance opposed to it is declining.

> Now a similar social process—in the last analysis the same social process—undermines the role and, along with the role, the social position of the capitalist entrepreneur. His role, though less glamorous than that of medieval warlords, great or small, also is or was just another form of individual leadership acting by virtue of personal force and personal responsibility for success. His position, like that of warrior classes, is threatened as soon as this function in the social process loses its importance, and no less if this is due to the cessation of the social needs it served than if those needs are being served by other, more impersonal, methods. (Schumpeter 1942, 133–134).

The decline of the entrepreneurial function and entrepreneurs, according to Schumpeter, opened the doors to the end of "capitalism" as we know it. Economic progress becomes depersonalized and automated, while committees and planning offices replaced individual action. The result, Schumpeter (1942, 134) stressed, may not differ from what Marxist scientists describe: *de facto* socialism.

3. KIRZNER: ENTREPRENEUR'S ALERTNESS TO PROFIT OPPORTUNITIES

While *Theorie der wirtschaftlichen Entwicklung* is the book that has to be studied in order to grasp the Schumpeterian vision about entrepreneurship, Kirzner's central work on the topic is *Competition and Entrepreneurship* (Kirzner, 1973). In a way, the starting point for the authors is not radically different. In the first chapter of *Theorie*, Schumpeter described the circular flow, a static economic system "ruled" by Walrasian scientific laws; then the Austrian economist shifted his focus, explaining that such a system is inadequate to grasp the dynamic nature of capitalistic development. In a similar way, Kirzner started by explaining why the neoclassical static mainstream is not the proper paradigm to analyze the competitive process (Kirzner 2000, 60–11). In fact, Kirzner's theory of entrepreneurship is part of a more general reflection devoted to competition as a process (the market process), in which entrepreneurs play a key role.

Kirzner's starting point is a "dissatisfaction with the usual emphasis on *equilibrium analysis*" and the "attempt to replace this emphasis by a fuller understanding of the operation of the market as a *process*" (Kirzner 1973, 1). According to the mainstream, in fact, the main task of price theory is to bring out a set of prices and quantities consistent with equilibrium conditions[2]. On the contrary, the Austrian economist tried to:

> [. . .] look to price theory to help us understand how the decisions of individual participants in the market interact to generate the market forces which compel changes in prices, in outputs, and in methods of production and the allocation of resources. [...] The efficiency of the price system, in this approach, does not depend upon the optimality (or absence of it) of the resource allocation pattern at equilibrium; rather, it depends on the degree of success with which market forces can be relied upon to generate spontaneous corrections in the allocation patterns prevailing at times of disequilibrium. (Kirzner 1973, 6–7).

The "original sin" of neoclassical mainstream, in Kirzner's view, is to refer to competition as "a state of affairs." We all studied, in our

---

[2] Kirzner (1997, 61): "At the basis of this approach is the conviction that standard neoclassical microeconomics, for which the Walrasian general equilibrium model [...] is the analytical core, fails to offer a satisfying theoretical framework for understanding what happens in the market economies."

microeconomics textbooks, that *perfect competition*, by definition, is a state of affairs in which economic players are characterized by perfect knowledge, perfect foresight, and, moreover, behave as price-takers[3]: The players are so many that nobody can actually influence the price level. Moreover, technology, tastes, and preferences, together with expectations, are given, and they are not subject to an internal impulse toward modification.

Finally, in the neoclassical perfect competition, the time dimension is missing. It is self-evident that this definition describes "the opposite of its meaning either in ordinary language or in common sense economic discussions of competition" (O'Driscoll and Rizzo 1985, 124).

In order to develop his entrepreneurial theory, therefore, Kirzner (1963, 3) first sought to redesign a market theory to set up the framework in which entrepreneurs act and move. This is probably the Kirzner's major contribution to the Austrian School of Economics: to build upon Mises's[4] and Hayek's[5] legacy an organic theory of the market as an economic *process* (Kirzner 1997, 61). Consumers, entrepreneur/producers, and resource owners are the players in the market; the market, in turn, is where their interacting decisions, during any period of time, take place. Every player has their own content of (limited) knowledge, tastes, and expectations. Depending on their knowledge, tastes, and expectations, the players set up their actions, decisions, or plans. Since, in order to carry out their plans, individuals need to interact, it is only through interaction and over time that the content of information will be modified and eventually a revision of decisions can happen:

> [. . .] During the given period of time, exposure to the decisions of others communicates some of the information these decision-makers originally lacked. If they find that their plans cannot be carried out, this teaches them that their anticipations concerning the decisions of others were overly optimistic. Or they may learn that their undue pessimism has caused them to pass up attractive market opportunities[6]. This newly

---

[3] As stated in Kirzner (2000, 13), in such a system, rivalry, which is the essence of competition, is absent.

[4] In particular referring to the concept of human action as purposeful action.

[5] In particular with regard to the theory of information transmission and coordination in the market via price mechanism.

[6] Also Schumpeter (1947, 157) emphasized the entrepreneurial attention to profit opportunities, but with a different emphasis: "The entrepreneurial performance involves, on the one hand, the ability to perceive new opportunities that cannot be proved at the moment at which action has to be taken, and, on the other hand, will power adequate to break down the resistance that the social environment offers to change." For Schumpeter, such opportunities cannot be proved, while for Kirzner they are consistent in a means-ends framework.

acquired information concerning the plans of others can be expected to generate, for the succeeding period of time, *a revised set of decisions.* (Kirzner 1973, 10).

As defined by Kirzner (1973, 10), then, market process is built up by "this series of systematic changes in the interconnected network of market decisions." Therefore, it is not possible to conceive a market process in the realm of perfect knowledge. The process arises precisely because of the initial ignorance of market participants and the natural uncertainty of human action. And the process can only happen during the flow of *real time.* With no market ignorance and no review of plans, there is no process at all. Starting with the Misesian concept of purposeful action, and building on the Hayekian insight of the market process as a process through which players' plans become more consistent with each other, Kirzner explained the *competitive nature* of such a process: Since from one period of market ignorance to the next one, ignorance has been somewhat reduced, market participants realize that not only should they implement more attractive opportunities but also that such attractiveness needs to be judged in comparison with the opportunities offered by competitors (Kirzner, 1973, p. 12). When the incentive to offer more attractive opportunities stops, the competitive process stops too, while the neoclassical equilibrium theory systematically ignores the "dynamic rivalry" constituting competition Kirzner (1997, 68). In a situation of market equilibrium, such as the one described by the neoclassical theory of perfect competition, there is no room for competition at all.

In describing such a process, almost incidentally and initially imagining a fictional world in which market participants are unable to learn from their experience, Kirzner (1973, 14) introduced a special group of individuals, who "*are* able to perceive opportunities for entrepreneurial profits; that is, they are able to see where a good can be sold at a price higher than that for which it can be bought." These are *entrepreneurs,* who "immediately notice profit opportunities *that exist because of the initial ignorance of the original market participants*" (Kirzner 1973, 14). Of course, to describe the real market process it is not necessary to divide the actors into two rigid groups, one that cannot learn from experience and the other one (entrepreneurial) which instead can. It is realistic, indeed, to introduce the entrepreneurial aspect as an element of the activities of each market participant. It follows that the market process is essentially entrepreneurial (Kirzner 1973, 15): since *entrepreneurship* is *alertness* to profit opportunities deriving from market ignorance, and the market process is the set of revisions in plans following the modification of knowledge, the two concept are intrinsically bounded.

It is only after the brief introduction of the concept of entrepreneurship in the realm of the market process that Kirzner moves on to detail his perspective about the entrepreneur. The first important note that the Austrian economist brought out is that entrepreneurship is related to human action and is therefore present, potentially, in each individual (Kirzner 1973, 31). In particular, as Kirzner developed the market process notion in opposition to an equilibrium approach, the author contrasted entrepreneurial activity with economizing and maximizing functions.

> [. . .] It is my position that this analytical vision of economizing, maximizing, or efficiency-intent individual market participants is, in significant respects, misleadingly incomplete. It has led to a view of the market as made up of a multitude of economizing individuals, each making his decisions with respect to *given* series of ends and means. [...] A multitude of economizing individuals each choosing with respect to given ends and means cannot, without the introduction of further exogenous elements, generate a market process (which involves systematically *changing* series of means available to market participants). (Kirzner 1973, 32–33).

The important point raised up by Kirzner is that, in such an analytical framework, in which ends and means are given, there is no room to study *how* ends and means are decided. To overcome the economizing notion, he went back to Mises's concept of *human action*. It is necessary to quote Kirzner's words in full:

> [. . .] Instead of economizing, I maintain, it will prove extremely helpful to emphasize the broader Misesian notion of *human action*. As developed by Mises, the concept of *homo agens* is capable of all that can be achieved by using the notions of economizing and of the drive for efficiency. But the human-action concept, unlike that of allocation and economizing, does not confine decision–maker (or the economic analysis of his decisions) to a framework of *given* ends and means. Human action, in the sense developed by Mises, involves courses of action taken by the human being "to remove uneasiness" and to make himself "better off." Being broader than the notion of economizing, the concept of human action does not restrict analysis of the decision to the allocation problem posed by the juxtaposition of scarce means and multiple ends. The

decision, in the framework of the human–action approach, is not arrived at merely by mechanical computation of the solution to the maximization problem implicit in the configuration of the given ends and means. It reflects not merely the manipulation of given means to correspond faithfully with the hierarchy of given ends, but also *the very perception of the ends-mean framework* within which allocation and economizing is to take place. (Kirzner 1973, 33).

While Robbins's economizing man can only react in a given way to a strictly defined set of ends and means, Misesian *homo agens* can *also* identify which ends to strive for and which means are available. This is possible because human beings can actually "*imagine* the future, even a non-existent, unknowable future" (Kirzner 1992, 25). Instead, economizing behavior does not take into account the process of identifying ends and means. It is at this point that Kirzner specifically introduced his famous concept of *alertness*[7] to "possibly newly worthwhile goals and to possibly newly available resources" (Kirzner, 1973, p. 35); such alertness is what is labelled the *entrepreneurial element* in human decision-making. If entrepreneurship is alertness, thus, the succession of different decisions, and their revisions, can be seen as a sequence of linked actions, the fruit of the learning process due to alertness (Kirzner 1973, 36). In a way, the concept of alertness is linked with *discovery* and *surprise*: profit opportunities do not "fall from the sky" but neither do entrepreneurs deliberately look for them:

> [. . .] The profit opportunities created by earlier entrepreneurial error do tend systematically to stimulate subsequent entrepreneurial discovery. The entrepreneurial process so set into motion, is a process tending toward better mutual awareness among market participants. The lure of pure profit in this way sets up the process through which pure profit tends to be competed away. Enhanced mutual awareness, via the entrepreneurial discovery process, is the source of the market's equilibrative properties. (Kirzner 1997, 72).

From this Kirzner derived his concept of the *pure entrepreneur*. For Schumpeter the action that identifies the pure entrepreneur is to bring out new combinations; for Kirzner (1973, 39) he or she is "a decision-maker whose *entire* role arises out of his alertness to hitherto unnoticed opportunities." For

---

[7] Sometimes called also *awareness*. As explained in Kirzner (1963, 42), entrepreneurs are aware, before others, of the discrepancies between prices that can generate profits.

both the economists, in fact, entrepreneurship is completely independent of the ownership of the means of production. The entrepreneurial function is, instead, strictly related to a special attitude: introducing new combinations (action) for Schumpeter, alertness (pre-action) for Kirzner. Regarding alertness, however, a clarification becomes necessary: The Kirznerian entrepreneur does *not* possess a greater knowledge. On the contrary, alertness is defined as "*the* *"knowledge" of where to find market data*" (Kirzner 1973, 67). Therefore, the Kirznerian type of entrepreneurship is in no way related to a certain kind of superiority but consists *only* in ""knowing where to look for knowledge" rather than knowledge of substantive market information" (Kirzner 1973, 68); this is the reason why Kirzner did not label this attitude *knowledge* but *alertness*.

The most distinctive feature of the Kirznerian entrepreneurial function is to move the market from a disequilibrium status toward equilibrium (Kirzner 1973, 69–75). The starting point of human action, in fact, is always a state of disequilibrium, characterized by market ignorance. As we already noticed, it is through interaction in the market that knowledge can be transmitted and acquired, bringing out revisions to plans. Entrepreneurial alertness allows such changes to happen and, therefore, reducing market-ignorance and driving plans toward mutual compatibility, it is an *equilibrating* force. The market approach, in fact, focuses "on the role of knowledge and discovery in the process of market equilibration. In particular this approach (a) sees equilibration as a systematic process in which market participants acquire more and more accurate and complete *mutual knowledge* of potential demand and supply attitudes, and (b) sees the driving force behind this systematic process in what will be described below as *entrepreneurial discovery*" (Kirzner 1997, 62).

The equilibrating process consists exactly in the acquisition of better mutual information concerning the plans made by different market actors.[8] It is only in disequilibrium that profit opportunities actually exist and can be discovered by entrepreneurial alertness.[9] In this sense, alertness allows

---

[8] In the market economy the problem of coordination finds solution in the market process and the key role is played by prices. (Kirzner 1963, 38).

[9] "For Austrians [...] mutual knowledge is indeed full of gaps at any given time, yet the market process is understood to provide a systemic set of forces, set in motion by entrepreneurial alertness, which tend to reduce the extent of mutual ignorance. Knowledge is not perfect; but neither is ignorance necessarily invincible. Equilibrium is indeed never attained, yet the market does exhibit powerful tendencies toward it." (Kirzner 1992, 5).

discovery, and discovery plays an equilibrating role, reducing market-ignorance (Kirzner 1997, 68).

Finally, as for Schumpeter entrepreneurial profit comes from the essence of entrepreneurial function (introducing new combinations); for Kirzner it is a consequence of alertness:

> [. . .] The pure entrepreneur […] proceeds by his alertness to discover and exploit situation in which he is able to sell for high prices that which he can buy for low prices. Pure entrepreneurial profit is the difference between the two set of prices. It is not yielded by exchanging something the entrepreneur values less for something he values more highly. It comes from discovering sellers and buyers of something for which the latter will pay more than the former demand. The discovery of a profit opportunity *means the discovery of something obtainable for nothing at all*. No investment at all is required. (Kirzner 1973, 48).

For Kirzner, too, entrepreneurs can obtain their resources from capitalists (this is another common element with Schumpeter), and profit must be kept separate from interest.

4. A COMPARISON: COMMON ELEMENTS AND DIFFERENCES

It is now time to see if there are elements to find common features to reduce the gap that seems to separate the two economists.[10] The analysis accomplished in this paragraph is the door to develop a new vision about entrepreneurship in the next section.

As I already had occasion to notice, both Schumpeter and Kirzner started showing a sort of delusion with respect to the neoclassical equilibrium approach. The first chapter of *Theorie* is devoted to the description of the circular flow (or what Mises (1949, 245–251) called "the evenly rotating economy"), an economic system which, repeating itself, can be studied with a static approach to economics. However, Schumpeter claimed to be interested in a different analysis, for which the circular flow method is not adequate:

---

[10] Kirzner himself is constantly concerned about the comparison between his view and Schumpeter's. See Kirzner (1973, 79–81; 1999; 2008).

The theory of the first chapter describes economic life from the standpoint of a "circular flow," running on in channels essentially the same year after year—similar to the circulation of the blood in an animal organism. Now, this circular flow and its channels do alter in time, and here we abandon the analogy with the circulation of the blood. For although the latter also changes in the course of the growth and decline of the organism, yet it only does so continuously, that is by steps which one can choose smaller than any assignable quantity, however small, and always within the same framework. Economic life experiences such changes too, but it also experiences others which do not appear continuously and which change the framework, the traditional course itself. They cannot be understood by means of any analysis of the circular flow [...]. Now such changes and the phenomena which appear in their train are the object of our investigation. [...] How do such changes take place, and to what economic phenomena do they give rise? (Schumpeter 1934, 61–62).

In a similar way, Kirzner did not deny *in toto* validity for the general economic equilibrium approach, but he judged it not to be enough for the analysis of the market approach. The first common element that thus needs to be stressed is the dissatisfaction with the static neoclassical approach; it is this dissatisfaction that moved both authors toward dynamic theories. And it is in the realm of these dynamic theories that Schumpeter and Kirzner gave life to their entrepreneurs.

Such dissatisfaction is used by the two economists to move toward dynamic theories. However, their theories are different: development theory centered on the carrying out of new combination for Schumpeter; dynamic market process focused on knowledge and market ignorance reduction for Kirzner. As we shall see, Schumpeterian development theory is the analysis of economic change dynamically built on the role of entrepreneur-innovators as special human types. Kirznerian market process, on the contrary, is carried out by human action that does not require leaders or special human beings.

In any case, in both development theory and market process theory, entrepreneurs play a crucial role. Both Schumpeterian and Kirznerian entrepreneurs arise as human types opposed to something else. We know that for Schumpeter entrepreneurs are special human types with a peculiar function; as I already pointed out, Schumpeterian entrepreneurs not only bring out new combinations, driving economic change; they are, also and above all, leaders able to master economic change, to dare where normal individuals stop, facing social and economic opposition and finally winning their challenge. Such a special human type is opposed to normal individuals, the static ones, who can only promptly react to well-known economic conditions. We can consider the static type analyzed by Schumpeter as the Robbinsian economizing man to which Kirzner opposes his *homo agens*.[11] If the economizing man can simply make rational decisions before given ends and means, Kirznerian *homo agens* is also able to set his ends-means framework and modify it while acquiring knowledge through market interactions; each *homo agens* is endowed with "propensity for alertness toward fresh goals and the discovery of hitherto unknown resources" (Kirzner 1973, 34).

At this point I must insert a big "but." Even if we have to recognize both the Schumpeterian innovator and the Kirznerian *homo agens* as opposed to the Robbinsian static economizing man, the degree to which they are opposed is different. Schumpeter is talking about two kinds of men that actually exist; Kirzner, instead, is explaining two facets of a process. For the older economist, an entrepreneurial leader is a different human being, opposed to static men; he is talking of two different categories of beings. In contrast, in Kirzner the opposition is lighter: To be *homo agens* is not something set against economizing activity; rather, after we "identify the ends–means framework which *homo agens* perceives as relevant, we can analyze his decision in orthodox Robbinsian allocation-economizing terms" (Kirzner 1973, 34). This means that Kirzner did not distinguish two kinds of human beings but two different stages in human actions. Each acting man needs *first* the entrepreneurial element called alertness to "possibly newly worthwhile goals and to possibly newly available resources in order to identify his means-ends framework; economizing activity is possible *as consequence* of such identification. However, to mark his difference with the neoclassical paradigm, Kirzner explained that ends and means are not given once and forever; as time flows, interaction and alertness can force revision of previous frameworks, bringing out new ones with different, and new, economizing decisions.

With regard to this point, one more thing should be noted: For Schumpeter *not* everybody is potentially an entrepreneur. Leadership and propensity to change are features of a specific human type, different from the static type. For Kirzner, instead, entrepreneurship, defined as alertness to unnoticed profit opportunities, is potentially present in every man. In this sense, as explained in Huerta de Soto (1992), human action and entrepreneurship are strictly related.

---

[11] "The distinction which Schumpeter draws at length between the way men would act in "the accustomed circular flow" on the one hand and when "confronted by a new task" on the other is closely parallel to my own distinction between "Robbinsian" decision-making and entrepreneurial activity." (Kirzner 1973, 79–80).

Entrepreneurship is necessary to everybody in order to set the means-ends framework; not everybody is alert with regard to the same profit opportunities at the same time; but alertness is a necessary element for human action regardless. Moreover, while Schumpeterian entrepreneurship, as an attitude toward change, is temporary by nature and, in the same man, will exhaust its power after a certain period of time, Kirznerian entrepreneurship, as basic feature of human action, needs to always be present, to a certain extent, during the lifecyle.

Turning now to what it seems to be the biggest difference between Schumpeter and Kirzner, we have to talk about the role of entrepreneurs with reference to equilibrium condition.

> Schumpeter's entrepreneur, I pointed out, was essentially disruptive, *destroying the pre-existing state of equilibrium*. My entrepreneur, on the other hand, was responsible for the tendency through which initial conditions of disequilibrium come systematically to be displaced by *equilibrative* market competition. (Kirzner 1999, 5).

Under this perspective, it seems that the two economists' positions are distant. For Schumpeter, the starting condition for the study of economic development is equilibrium. Entrepreneurs, bringing out new combinations, break such equilibrium, moving the economic system somewhere else. In Kirzner, instead, we have the opposite consideration. The starting point is a disequilibrium situation, due to market ignorance; the entrepreneurial role is an equilibrating one. As entrepreneurial function is alertness to previously unnoticed profit opportunities, it reduces market ignorance, helping individual plans to become more mutually consistent. Therefore, in Kirzner entrepreneurship is an equilibrating force, while according to Schumpeter its very nature is to break with equilibrium, a state in which change is not happening. However, if we look at the role of innovation as conceived by Schumpeter (1939) and strictly related with business cycles, we find that, if initially new combinations break with the previous equilibrium state, crisis is identified as a path toward a *new* equilibrium situation (Ferlito 2013, 67–68). As soon as entrepreneurial impetus loses steam pulling the system away from its previous area of equilibrium, the system embarks on a struggle toward a new equilibrium.

In short, if in Kirzner, entrepreneurship is *essentially* an equilibrating force, for Schumpeter, while moving the system away from the previous area of equilibrium, it gives rise to a process (business cycle) in which the last phase is the struggle toward a new equilibrium. Therefore we can observe that for both the economists the entrepreneurial function is the trigger for two processes (market process in Kirzner, development and business cycle in Schumpeter) in which equilibrating forces operate. In Kirzner's vision they consists in the ignorance reduction driven by entrepreneurial discovery. According to Schumpeter, instead, they identify with the liquidation crisis following a boom initiated by entrepreneurial, innovative action.

Turning to the methodological perspective, instead, Schumpeter and Kirzner are children of two different approaches. While Kirzner is *fully* part of the Austrian tradition in economics, Schumpeter cannot be considered part of any school; at the same time he did not generate one. If influences on Schumpeter would be found, they need to be sought in some members of the German historical school: Sombart, Weber and, in particular, Schumpeter's great friend Arthur Spiethoff. Schumpeter was not interested in bringing out universally valid, economic laws; rather, his attempt was to describe the economic and social evolution *in the historical time*. The Schumpeterian entrepreneur, thus, plays his role in a well-determined historical context; and, in fact, moving from *Theorie* to *Business Cycles* and, finally, *Capitalism, Socialism and Democracy*, Schumpeter did not substantially change his description of entrepreneurship, but he was conscious that the historical role of entrepreneurs *as persons* was changing (Ebner 2006, 324–328). In Kirzner, instead, such historical context is missing. Following Misesian praxeology,[12] his attempt was to identify "universal" laws of human action, elements that remain constant as a natural part of human behavior. Kirznerian entrepreneurship is not an historical phenomenon, responsible for a specific stage of economic development, as the Schumpeterian *personal* entrepreneur is. To debate who is right is not necessary: Talking about entrepreneurship, Schumpeter and Kirzner described two different things. Their methodological approach is consistent with their vision; so, in a sense, they are both right.

5. ENTREPRENEURSHIP AND CAPITAL: A NEW SYNTHESIS

In drawing up my concluding remarks, I wish to repeat first of all that Schumpeter's and Kirzner's entrepreneurial theories both arose in opposition

---

[12] Praxeology "takes as its fundamental premise the existence of human action. Once it is demonstrated that human action is a necessary attribute of the existence of human beings, the rest of praxeology (and its subdivision, economic theory) consists of the elaboration of the logical implications of the concept of action." (Rothbard 1962, 72).

to neoclassical equilibrium theory. What the two economists brought out from such opposition are two analyses of human behavior driving the economic system in certain directions.

Schumpeter's entrepreneur, maker and master of change, is a *deus ex machina* for capitalistic economic development. A very specific period of economic history is related with his function: the era of "heroic" leader entrepreneurs characterizing the eighteenth, nineteenth, and the beginning of the twentieth centuries. As historical conditions change (*trustification*), the role of entrepreneurs changes too, while *the responsibility* of forging economic development through "new combinations' shifts to research centrers and managers.

Kirznerian entrepreneurship, instead, is not conceived as a historical matter or a specific characteristics of "superior men." Rather, it is a general feature of human action, consisting in the possibility to set up a means-ends framework in order to exploit unnoticed profit opportunities. Under this perspective, everybody is potentially entrepreneurial, through time and space. Space and time conditions do not change the general feature of entrepreneurship, which remains a constant element of human beings behavior through centuries. Kirznerian entrepreneurs are not the "prime cause" of economic development; instead, through their alertness, they generate the market process as a process of information exchange and therefore ignorance reduction. Alertness becomes an equilibrating force helping economic actors in making their plans mutually consistent.

My perspective is that *both* entrepreneurial ideas can coexist when looking at a definition of entrepreneurship consistent with our hermeneutical approach to capital theory. The source of misunderstanding, I believe, is that the two economists labelled different concepts with the same word. The Schumpeterian entrepreneur is not incompatible with the Kirznerian one. I agree with the theory of human action described by Kirzner, but it seems too weak to fully explain the essence of entrepreneurship. Kirzner's theory can be the first brick in an integrated human action and entrepreneurship theory if we renounce labeling it as entrepreneurial theory, and we simply call it *alertness theory*. Markets are characterized by ignorance and economic agents define their sets of ends and means consistently with their expectations and the limited content of their knowledge. In doing so, they trigger the market process and the never-ending processes of information exchange and revising plans. They are alert to profit opportunities, and they learn from experience.

However, among these economic actors, *special types* can actually arise. The introduction of new combinations and the leadership attitudes do not need to be excluded by Kirzner's model. Schumpeter's entrepreneurs arise from Kirznerian alertness, driving the economic system toward *change*. New combinations can be seen, thus, as a subset of the general human action, a special kind of action bringing into the market process, in terms of *change*, something stronger that what is previously known. Similarly, Schumpeterian entrepreneurs are fully consistent with the human action model. They are alert to unnoticed profit opportunities, and they need to set up their ends-means frameworks. In doing so, however, the kind of plans and the set of actions they carry out, not being theoretically different from all the other kinds of actions, are practically different for the special consequences they bring into the economic system. In fact, such actions introduce radical discontinuities in the way to do things[13].

The disruptive character of Schumpeterian entrepreneurs and the coordinative role as described by Kirzner are, therefore, not entirely inconsistent. Looking at the system from the outside, Schumpeter's entrepreneur shows us the importance of technological change for economic evolution. Kirzner's insights, instead, enlighten the working of the economic system from the inside (the arising of profit opportunities from ignorance and alertness as possibility to crab them) (Kirzner 1999, 16).

It seems that recently Kirzner (1999) became aware of the potential "cooperation" between the two visions.[14] In particular, and this is consistent with my perspective, Kirzner (1999, 5) stressed how Schumpeter's view is valid in order to understand "the psychological profile typical of the real-world entrepreneur" and the ''creative destruction" which Schumpeter saw as the central and distinguishing feature of the "capitalist" system. Kirzner (1999, 12) recognized that alertness requires "boldness, self-confidence, creativity and innovative ability" as described by Schumpeterian entrepreneurship. Moreover it seems that the Austrian economist also accepted the special psychological attitude necessary for entrepreneurship typical of the Schumpeter's vision.[15]

Schumpeterian entrepreneurship (characterized by leadership and innovation) can be seen as a special action arising from the Austrian

---

[13] Kirzner (1992, 50) probably moved toward my vision, stating that "entrepreneurship exercised in innovative production tents to generate technological progress."

[14] Kirzner (2008, 8) pointed out that the "merely alert entrepreneur [...] was never intended as alternative to the creative, innovative Schumpeterian entrepreneur."

[15] Kirzner (1999, 13): "abstract prescience [must] be supported by psychological qualities that encourage one to ignore conventional wisdom, to dismiss the jeers of those deriding what they see as the self-deluded visionary, to disrupt what other have come to see as the comfortable familiarity of the old-fashioned ways of doing things, to ruin rudely and even cruelly the confident expectations of those whose somnolence has led them to expect to continue to make their living as they have for years past."

(Kirznerian) concept of human action, but brought out by special human types, entrepreneurs, and with radical consequences not simply for the market process but for the economic development process.

We can imagine an *alertness* (Kirznerian) theory in which human beings, as *homo agens*, define their ends-means framework and their plans. Interaction between these *homo agens* is defining market process, characterized by ignorance reduction and plans revision and coordination. Among such plans, some are *entrepreneurial*, disruptive plans (''new combinations''), brought out by Schumpeterian entrepreneurs and defining economic change.

Relating all this to our capital theory, we note how all individuals are involved in capital formation as part of the alertness processes advocated by Kirzner. The hermeneutical moment described in Chapter 1 involves all human beings when they try to define an ends-means framework consistent with their expectations. From this perspective, capital formation, intended as the choice and implementation of goods combination in order to fulfill expectations, is inherent in all human actions. However, as implied above, we cannot conclude that capital formation processes, as human actions, uniquely define entrepreneurship, which I believe to be a smaller category.

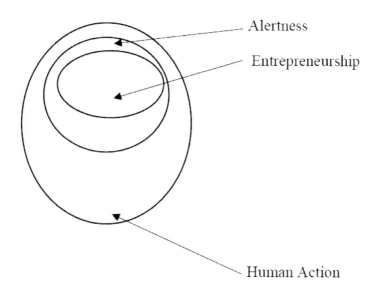

Figure 1. Human Action, Alertness and Entrepreneurship.

As represented in Figure 1, both alertness and entrepreneurship are subsets of human action, and both imply capital formation, intended as potential and actual capital. It must be clear, moreover, that entrepreneurship and alertness do not have to be distinguished by whether they are carried out by firms or individuals; this does not matter. What marks the difference between the two phenomena are the consequences brought about by the implementation of goods combinations. With this definition, I feel closer to Schumpeter than Kirzner. The choice to give birth to production processes involving a goods combination is an everyday experience of the economic activity. However, the implementation of *certain* capital combination brings about radical consequences for the economic system that can be judged only *ex post*.

At the hermeneutical moment there is no difference between alertness and entrepreneurship. In both cases, a choice happens among available goods in order to fulfill expectations dictated by the subjective impact of active minds with the surrounding objective reality. The trigger is the attempt, by the individual, to move toward an improved situation (profit, broadly intended). But, remember formula (8):

$$O_x = F(O_n; AC; tf) \tag{8}$$

The production process output is a function not only of the time flow and of the actual capital. Above all, it is a function of expectations (in a non-deterministic way). It is therefore clear that the possibility for a plan to achieve certain consequences for the economic system is defined at a pre-hermeneutical moment and precisely when expectations are formed. In most cases, the definition of expectations as potentially able to bring about a radical transformation in the economic system qualifies itself as an unconscious process: Entrepreneurs do not necessarily intend to be "revolutionary," they are moved simply by the desire for profit. But somehow some of them define expectations able to carry out capital combinations which will generate an output able to bring a discontinuity in the "mode of production," a discontinuity such as the one defined for the "new combinations" by Schumpeter.

It must be noted that the possibility for expectations and capital to generate such a radical impact is not unequivocally determined by intrinsic features of expectations and capital in themselves. The final outcome will be determined by the unexhausted flow of changes happening in the time flow and by the institutional context in which production processes take place.

To summarize: *Alertness capital formation processes* can be defined as the choice of goods combination in order to bring out an output able to fulfill expectations. They are a subset of human actions. Among the different production processes set in motion by individual alertness, some of them will be able to generate an output which will mark a permanent discontinuity in the economic system, such as the one brought out by Schumpeterian new combinations. The possibility for such an outcome to happen is defined by the original expectations, by the implementation of capital combination, by the continuous flow of novelty brought out by time flow, and by the institutional framework.

$$EO = F(O_n;AC;tf;I) \tag{9}$$

Where *EO* is the entrepreneurial outcome and *I* is the institutional framework. In this sense entrepreneurship can be judged only *ex post*; it is defined by its consequences and not by some characteristics identifiable before any production process is implemented. Entrepreneurship is, thus, an unintended consequence, falling into what Hayek (1967, 96-105) called the result of human action but not of human design.

Of course, I cannot define entrepreneurship as a totally casual phenomenon, and this is the reason why I brought out formula (9), which again must be intended in a non-deterministic way. Some individuals are able to form expectations (O_n) and to combine, accordingly, some actual capital goods (*AC*) which, in the time flow and in the realm of a certain institutional context, can generate radical consequences for the economic system. At which extent does the possibility for such a revolutionary outcome to be generated depend on "superhuman" features in the sense advocated by Schumpeter? I suggest that entrepreneurial outputs are the combined result of many factors and that special, human or superhuman, characteristics are not enough to explain the emergence or extraordinary consequences.

Being dependent of expectations, entrepreneurial outcomes for sure involves the formation of *entrepreneurial expectations*, in the sense that such expectations must contain in themselves the seed for a potential extraordinary result. The possibility for such special expectations to arise, in turn, needs to be related to a special vision, to the ability to imagine, for certain potential outputs, the possibility to generate extraordinary profit opportunities. I argue that such a vision is partially consciously and partially unconsciously present in entrepreneurial spirits. However, the vision is not enough. I already mentioned the importance of the institutional context. And, above all, *real* entrepreneurs manifest themselves in the ability to imagine (*PC*) and implement the right goods combinations (*AC*) which will be able to generate the desired outcome.

Entrepreneurship, as mentioned, can be judged only *ex post* from the result. The same holds true for entrepreneurs, whose features remain hidden until the outcome of their capital combinations is revealed.

Chapter 3

CAPITAL, EXPECTATIONS, AND BUSINESS CYCLES: THE *NATURAL CYCLE*

1. INTRODUCTION: ON THE INEVITABILITY OF ECONOMIC FLUCTUATIONS

The economic crisis that erupted in 2007 led Austrian economists to revive the Austrian Business Cycle Theory (ABCT) and to point a finger at the distortive actions taken by government intervention and in particular by central banks.[1] The most interesting fact emerging from the post-crisis economic debate is maybe that, while neoclassical mainstream is suffering, old heterodox schools are trying to revive themselves and face a growing consensus. From this perspective it has become clear that the Hayek/Keynes debate is far from defunct. Disciples of the two great economists are still in the boxing ring.[2]

The first point I will bring out here is that economic crises do not demonstrate the end of the free market economic system; on the contrary, they testify to its vitality. In Ferlito (2013, 30) and in Ferlito (2014), I tried to demonstrate that economic development without fluctuations does not exist.[3] Indeed, I find myself in good company in believing that the cycle is the real

---

[1] Among the others, see Prychitko (2010), Salerno (2012), Hülsmann (2013), Ferlito (2013) and Koppl (2014).

[2] See Ferlito (2015b).

[3] Huerta de Soto (1998, 468) pointed out that "[o]ne of the more curious points on which a certain agreement exists [between Marxian and Austrian analysis] relates precisely to the theory of the crises and recessions which systematically ravage the capitalist system."

form of economic development (Ferlito 2011, 96). Marx was the first to realize this (Rothbard 1969, 13). The same awareness is to be seen in Schumpeter's vision, influenced by Spiethoff (1925, 112), who concluded that "the cyclical upswings and downswings are the evolutionary forms of the highly developed capitalist economy and their antithetic stimuli condition its progress."[4] In turn, the Austrian economist influenced his student Paolo Sylos Labini (1954, 12–14; 1984, 37 and 89), and similar considerations can be found in Lachmann (1956, 110–112). Realizing that the cyclic form is typical of modern economic development is also echoed in the words of another Italian economist, Marco Fanno (1931, 248–249).[5]

Supported by the testimony of such economists, I shall bring out the motivations which drove me to similar conclusions. The core of my analysis will be an accent on the role of expectations, time preferences, and innovation mechanisms. I will build my theory on the pillars of the ABCT; however, as I shall demonstrate, Mises's approach, supporting the thesis that crises happen only when monetary authorities intervene on the money supply needs to be overcome. Austrian tradition, in fact, distinguishes between sustainable and unsustainable booms; only in the latter situation do crises arise. Instead, I will argue that depressions always follow booms; the difference among them is only in intensity and duration. In order to support my view, I will abandon Mises's view and use Hayek's perspective as starting point instead. This perspective will be then integrated with key elements coming from Schumpeter and Lachmann.

2. METHODOLOGICAL INTERMEZZO: WHY MAINSTREAM ECONOMICS FAILS IN CYCLES FORECASTING

I believe that modern macroeconomics failed to understand economic fluctuations because it is a prisoner of a static paradigm (general economic equilibrium), founded on econometric predictions. However, crises cannot be understood within the equilibrium framework.

First of all it is thus necessary to define the nature of the object of investigation. Indeed, the method is imposed by the goal. This does not mean surrendering to indistinct, methodological relativism, but it is acknowledging that phenomena of reality are complex and varied in nature. The problem of

---

[4] See Ferlito (2015d).
[5] See Nardi Spiller (1993; 2000).

business cycles is, of course, a dynamic one. As all economic theory, it should be related to reality, to living human beings, dynamically acting in a specific time and space framework. The center of economic analysis, as widely argued in Chapter 1, is, therefore, human action. Dealing with real people is very different from dealing with phenomena in physics or chemistry or natural sciences in general.

In this context, it is evident that the proper perspective for studying dynamic economic phenomena is subjective. The first fact to be noted as regards studying individuals and their actions is that every gesture is guided by a principle of finality. Economists are thus faced by qualitatively very well defined elements: man and reality. They should be inspired by these elements, should allow themselves to be astonished by what happens. The essence of an economist's work lies in observing reality, without seeking to put it in a cage. The observation of reality helps identify certain dynamic trends that represent constants in human action. For example, as we have seen, the human action has a finalistic nature. That is not to say, as in the rationalist terms of the general equilibrium theory, that every subject maximizes units of utility in accordance with mathematical models. This is not what happens in reality. It is true, however, as a dynamic trend, that man acts to achieve goals. This sees the onset of relationships with the surroundings, people, things, and complex society in general. Economists may certainly analyze everything that individuals do within the dynamics of enterprise in search of attaining their objectives.

It is possible to study these dynamics but without any pretence of planning and without including attitudes that fall within strict and formal models. Explanations are possible, only they must be of a qualitative nature. And achieving this requires the right set of tools.

In conclusion, the business of the economic scientist is possible if the search of functional relations is replaced by the desire to really understand how reality works, abandoning every constructivist temptation determined by pseudo-scientific dazzle or the possibility of perfect planning.

3. THE TRADITIONAL VERSION OF THE ABCT: A SUMMARY

The most successful version of the ABCT is the one elaborated by Ludwig von Mises (1912, 1936, 1949), which can be summed up very simply: The first cause of the cyclical trend is the overexpansion of credit that may take the shape of an interest rate kept artificially low or the direct issue of money and its substitutes. In particular, *cheap money* encourages the appearance of economic initiatives that, under normal conditions, would not be judged viable. An economic system based on chance comes to the fore:

> [. . .] In issuing fiduciary media, by which I mean bank notes without gold backing or current accounts which are not entirely backed by gold reserves, the banks are in a position to expand credit considerably. The creation of these additional fiduciary media permits them to extend credit well beyond the limit set by their own assets and by the funds entrusted to them by their clients. They intervene on the market in this case as "suppliers" of additional credit, created by themselves, and they thus produce a lowering of the rate of interest, which falls below the level at which it would have been without their intervention. The lowering of the rate of interest stimulates economic activity. Projects which would not have been thought "profitable" if the rate of interest had not been influenced by the manipulations of the banks, and which, therefore, would not have been undertaken, are nevertheless found "profitable" and can be initiated. The more active state of business leads to increased demand for production materials and for labour. The prices of the means of production and the wages of labour rise, and the increase in wages leads, in turn, to an increase in prices of consumption goods. If the banks were to refrain from any further extension of credit and limited themselves to what they had already done, the boom would rapidly halt. But the banks do not deflect from their course of action; they continue to expand credit on a larger and larger scale, and prices and wages correspondingly continue to rise. (Mises1936, 28–29).

Yet this movement cannot continue indefinitely, since monetary means have expanded but the means of production and labor have not:

> [. . .] Society is not sufficiently rich to permit the creation of new enterprises without taking anything away from other enterprises. As long as the expansion of credit is continued this will not be noticed, but this extension cannot be pushed indefinitely. For if an attempt were made to prevent the sudden halt of the upward movement (and the collapse of prices which would result) by creating more and more credit, a continuous and even more rapid increase of prices would result. But the inflation and the boom can continue smoothly only as long as the public

thinks that the upward movement of prices will stop in the near future. As soon as public opinion becomes aware that there is no reason to expect an end to the inflation, and that prices will continue to rise, panic sets in. No one wants to keep his money; because its possession implies greater and greater losses from one day to the next; everyone rushes to exchange money for goods, people buy things they have no considerable use for without even considering the price, just in order to get rid of the money. (Mises 1936, 29–30).

As a consequence, product prices increase disproportionately.

[. . .] If, on the contrary, the banks decided to halt the expansion of credit in time to prevent the collapse of the currency and if a brake is thus put on the boom, it will quickly be seen that the false impression of "profitability" created by the credit expansion has led to unjustified investments. Many enterprises or business endeavours which had been launched thanks to the artificial lowering of the interest rate, and which had been sustained thanks to the equally artificial increase of prices, no longer appear profitable. Some enterprises cut back their scale of operation, others close down or fail. Prices collapse; crisis and depression follow the boom. The crisis and the ensuing period of depression are the culmination of the period of unjustified investment brought about by the extension of credit. The projects which owe their existence to the fact that they once appeared "profitable" in the artificial conditions created on the market by the extension of credit and the increase in prices which resulted from it, have ceased to be "profitable." The capital invested in these enterprises is lost to the extent that it is locked in. The economy must adapt itself to these losses and to the situation that they bring about. In this case the thing to do, first of all, is to curtail consumption and, by economizing, to build up new capital funds in order to make the productive apparatus conform to the actual wants and not to artificial wants which could never be manifested and considered as real except as a consequence of the false calculation of "profitability" based on the extension of credit. (Mises 1936, 30–31).

It can be seen how such explanatory system is diametrically opposed to the Keynesian paradigm, which views insufficient consumption as the cause of the crisis and emphasizes the need to stimulate consumption and aggregate demand in order to revive the system. Here, on the other hand, the formation of new savings is believed essential for such resumption. Even monetarist policies focusing on centralized manoeuvring of the interest rate are deemed ineffective for reviving the economy. Further reducing the interest rate, as central banks do today when a crisis breaks out, causes more harm than utility (Hayek 1929, 21–22).

> [. . .] Once the reversal of the trade cycle sets in following the change in banking policy, it becomes very difficult to obtain loans because of the general restriction of credit. The rate of interest consequently rises very rapidly as a result of a sudden panic. Presently it will fall again. It is a well-known phenomenon, indeed, that in a period of depressions a very low rate of interest-considered from the arithmetical point of view-does not succeed in stimulating economic activity. The cash reserves of individuals and of banks grow; liquid funds accumulate, yet the depression continues.
>
> [...]
>
> Finally, it will be necessary to understand that the attempts to artificially lower the rate of interest which arises on the market, through an expansion of credit, can only produce temporary results, and that the initial recovery will be followed by a deeper decline which will manifest itself as a complete stagnation of commercial and industrial activity The economy will not be able to develop harmoniously and smoothly unless all artificial measures that interfere with the level of prices, wages, and interest rates, as determined by the free play of economic forces, are renounced once and for all. It is not the task of the banks to remedy the consequences of the scarcity of capital or the effects of wrong economic policy by extension of credit. (Mises 1936, 32–35).

These are the essential features of the Austrian business cycle theory, as summarized by Ludwig von Mises himself. According to Rothbard (1969, 37), the cycle does not come to a halt because, at the end of a depression, the banks continue their expansionist approach and are crucially sustained in this approach by the state. Consequently, fluctuations are not the outcome of a failure of the market; on the contrary, they reflect the natural tendency of the state to stimulate credit expansion and inflation. The mass of entrepreneurial errors seen is caused by the artificial lowering of interest rates, which misleads entrepreneurs and promotes erroneous investments. Lastly, the (incorrect) perception among consumers of having a higher income because of inflation encourages them to spend the presumed additional income, thereby increasing demand for consumer goods to the detriment of demand for production goods.

4. TOWARD A NEW VISION: THE *NATURAL CYCLE*

Further evolutions of the ABCT explained that we should distinguish between *sustainable* and *unsustainable* boom. In both cases, the accent is on the modification of the intertemporal structure of preferences happening in one side of the economic system (consumers/savers or investors), which drives toward a modification of the natural interest rate[6] and of the intertemporal structure of production. In case of a *sustainable* boom no monetary manipulation happens, and economic agents are free to discover and coordinate their set of temporal preferences via the information transmission action operated by the specific price called "natural interest rate" and measuring the structure of the intertemporal preferences; such a boom is not followed by a bust. In the second case, instead, the existence of a monetary interest rate, set by monetary authorities, impedes the natural rate to play its role in information transmission and therefore the temporary discoordination in the structure of preferences remains. In such a situation, economic expansions are always followed by crises.

Using some of Hayek's intuitions, I shall try to demonstrate how such a version of the ABCT should be abandoned, in favor of a vision which sees crises as the *natural* outcome of *every* boom. We will therefore distinguish not between sustainable and unsustainable booms but between *monetary* cycles (the Austrian unsustainable boom/bust cycle) and the *natural* cycle, which starts as an Austrian sustainable boom but is followed by a liquidation crisis. In both cases, the starting point is the modification of the intertemporal structure of preferences. The two cycle stages can be described as follows:

---

[6] Hayek (1933, 145) stated that "an equilibrium rate of interest would then be one which assured correspondence between the intentions of the consumers and the intentions of the entrepreneurs. And with a constant rate of saving this would be the rate of interest arrived at on a market where the supply of money, capital was of exactly the same amount as current savings." In turn, Garrison (2006, 58–59) explained that "the natural rate [is] the rate that reflects the time preferences of market participants and allocates resources among the temporally defined stages of production. [...] In summary terms, the natural rate is seen as an equilibrium rate. It is the rate that tells the truth about the availability of resources for meeting present and future consumer demands, allowing production plans to be kept in line with the preferred pattern of consumption. By implication, an unnatural, or artificial, rate of interest is a rate that reflects some extra-market influence and that creates a disconnect between intertemporal consumption preferences and intertermporal production plans."

Table 2. Monetary Cycle vs Natural Cycle

	Monetary Cycle	Natural Cycle
Stage 1	Boom, ignited by a modification of the intertemporal structure of preferences. Price mechanism information transmission role blocked by monetary authority action.	Boom, ignited by a modification of the intertemporal structure of preferences. No monetary authority.
Stage 2	Secondary boom: Schumpeterian and imitation and speculation processes.	Secondary boom: Schumpeterian and imitation and speculation processes.
Stage 3	Crisis: liquidation of the secondary boom.	Crisis: liquidation of the secondary boom.
Stage 4	Depression: liquidation of most of the initiative initiated with stage 1.	

4.1. The Monetary Cycle

I shall now describe such cycles, with particular reference to the natural cycle as our most important theoretical novelty. Economic fluctuations are related with the modification of the intertemporal structure of preferences. At any given time, a time preference structure (summarized in the natural interest rate) is matched by a production structure, i.e., a heterogeneous set of combinations of capital goods, organized by human creative and entrepreneurial action in order to carry out processes that, over time, generate an output. This output should meet a demand defined by the structure of time preferences. This structure is reflected in an interest rate that, in turn, expresses the magnitude of the preference of economic agents for present goods compared to future goods.

The central point is the distortion of the production structure defined by the system of preferences (Hayek 1929, 123), and the reasons behind such a modification. The system of time preferences is determined by the expectations of players on the market who, following their own expectations, seek to implement plans to achieve them. In a free market system, this mechanism of action takes place through the meeting of different subjects who in the process acquire new information and change their expectations. We are therefore witnessing a gradual and continuous process of re-adaptation of plans, in a natural effort to ensure that their realization "meets" the realization of the plans of others.

The typical situation taken in account by Mises is when a natural rate is flanked by a monetary rate set by a central authority. In this scenario, the signal role played by the monetary rate overpowers that of the equilibrium rate, because it is immediately publicized and more visible to the players on the market: it "anticipates" the discovery mechanism typical of the market, it creates a wall between supply a demand. The monetary rate, inasmuch, becomes one of the essential engines driving profit expectations and the subsequent formation of plans. A difference between the natural rate and the monetary rate, by disorienting certain agents, may therefore modify the structure of production but without this change reflecting a parallel change in time preferences. Or, another possibility is that the monetary rate may not follow a unilateral change in preferences, thereby interfering with the process of adaptation by the economic system whose own preferences have not changed.

Let us now assume starting from a situation of equilibrium, a hypothetical starting point "0." We have a natural rate that reflects the meeting of time preferences and a production structure organised accordingly. Let's also suppose that the monetary rate set by central authorities is the same as the equilibrium rate. In this scenario, a disequilibrium between monetary rate and equilibrium value, whereby the former is at a value lower than the second, may arise in two ways. The first and most immediately intuitable hypothesis is that the central authorities cut the monetary rate in the belief that lowering the interest rate sets in motion an expansion cycle without negative repercussions. In such a scenario, central bank is misleading the profit expectations of entrepreneurs, wrongly informing them that new resources are available for investments. Therefore, entrepreneurs consider it is more convenient to invest in new investment projects, usually more time-consuming; however their choices are wrongly guided by a false signal, which, in "hiding" the natural rate, does not allow the system to activate the necessary counter-measures to the resurgence of natural tendencies toward equilibrium typical of a regime of freedom of entrepreneurial action. Entrepreneurs, following interest rate manipulation, become more future-oriented, although more savings are not generated; consequently, available resources are fictitious and time preferences are changed unilaterally, leading to a disequilibrium in intertemporal preferences; future-oriented investors and present-oriented consumers (or not as future-oriented as entrepreneurs). A change in time preferences always happens unilaterally, but when only the natural interest rate plays a role this change can be communicated to the other side of the market. The monetary interest rates does not allow the natural one to play is information transmission role.

Yet the situation whereby the monetary interest rate is below the natural rate may also occur without the intervention of central banks. In fact, the natural rate can be pushed upward by expanding profit expectations. Entrepreneurial action may be determined by so-called *sentiment*, the inkling that certain initiatives might be profitable. In this situation, entrepreneurs become future-oriented, raising the interest rate level and pushing demand for funds to begin the longer-term production processes.

> It is an apparently unimportant difference in exposition which leads one to this view that the Monetary Theory can lay claim to an endogenous position. The situation in which the money rate of interest is below the natural rate need not, by any means, originate in a deliberate lowering of the rate of interest by the banks. The same effect can be obviously produced by an improvement in the expectations of profit or by a diminution in the rate of saving, which may drive the "natural rate" (at which the demand for and the supply of savings are equal) above its previous level; while the banks refrain from raising their rate of interest to a proportionate extent, but continue to lend at the previous rate, and thus enable a greater demand for loans to be satisfied than would be possible by the exclusive use of the available supply of savings. (Hayek 1929, 147).

There can be many kinds of reasons for this.

> New inventions or discoveries, the opening up of new markets, or even bad harvests, the appearance of entrepreneurs of genius who originate 'new combinations' (Schumpeter), a fall in wage rates due to heavy immigration; and the destruction of great blocks of capital by a natural catastrophe or many others. We have already seen that none of these reasons is in itself sufficient to account for an *excessive* increase of investing activity, which necessarily engenders a subsequent crisis; but that they can lead to this result only through the increase in the means of credit which they inaugurate. (Hayek 1929, 168).

Even in this case, however, preferences change unilaterally. If, as it is, monetary rate, fixed by central banks, does not reflect the free market natural level and therefore it is not free to seek for an equilibrium level in order to encourage savers themselves to become more future-oriented by increasing saving amounts, the structure of preferences will remain disproportionate and the new intertemporal production structure will reflect such an imbalance. In this case, therefore, expectations change before the intervention of central banks: it is not monetary manipulation that plays the key role capable of altering the system of preferences by dis-coordinating plans and the structure of production. In the first situation, the crucial role is given by the manner and direction in which monetary expansion influence expectations. In the second case, on the other hand, expectations themselves divert the system away from equilibrium.

Changing expectations, caused by (case 1) or the cause of (case 2) a monetary rate below its natural level, is—on closer inspection—a natural part of the entrepreneurial instinct emphasized by Schumpeter. The analysis of the entrepreneurial role (innovation) as a fundamental element in initiating an expansion cycle, implemented in an organic way by Schumpeter, is entirely coherent with our analysis. We are explicitly discussing the concept of expectations: entrepreneurs see opportunities for profit and take advantage of them, i.e., they have positive expectations, or, otherwise, they are future-oriented and ready to make the production process more roundabout. Some are prepared to take risks on real innovations that can create a competitive advantage for them. Others by merely imitating on the wave of enthusiasm. Still others by launching poorly grounded economic initiatives.

Let's return now to our analysis and the disequilibrium between natural and monetary rates. The situation consideration therefore encourages the onset of major investments in long term projects, the production period is extended (Hayek 1931, 35–36). The cardinal point of the theory is the difference created between entrepreneurial decisions and consumer choices (Hayek 1933, 143–148). The funds available for investments initially do not correspond to the amount of savings. In fact, an artificially low monetary rate corresponds, on the capital market, to a higher availability of money because it translates into lower interest payable on investments.

> In general it is probably true to say that most investments are made in the expectation that the supply of capital will for some time continue at the present level. Or, in other words, entrepreneurs regard the present supply of capital and the present rate of interest as a symptom that approximately the same situation will continue to exist for some time. (Hayek 1933, 142).

What Hayek said is true, and the central role of expectations is resumed. Yet, all the more, the indicator on which entrepreneurs base their choices actually does not reflect any current propensity among consumers to save (Hayek 1933, 144). In this way, the proportion in which producers decide to differentiate production between products for the immediate future and those for the longer term (intertemporal production structure) does not reflect the way in which consumers intend to divide their income between savings and consumption (Hayek 1933, 144–145). It is evident that sooner or later a disequilibrium in time preferences, which is reflected in the inter-temporal production structure, will arise and the typical form will be the frustration of the expectations of one of the two groups (Lachmann 1943, 69 and Hayek 1933, 145).

So, while entrepreneurs invest in new long term processes, savers are frustrated in their desire to consume, because what they want is not being produced. The *forced saving* (Hayek, 1932) phenomenon thereby comes about, i.e.,—as a consequence of the fact that production resources were diverted from sectors close to consumers—there is a gradual reduction in the production of consumer goods and therefore an involuntary limitation of consumption (Kurz 2003, 191 and Hayek 1933, 145–146).

The entrepreneurial impetus toward new investments, on the other hand, initially involves an increase in raw material prices and consequently of the intermediate goods produced with them. And the impetus becomes particularly violent when the wave of the first innovative entrepreneurs is joined by the pressure of imitators described by Schumpeter, who grasp profit opportunities only in a second stage and attempt to benefit by following the "fashion." On a closer look, imitative speculation waves are typical of every boom stage described in history.

At the same time, demand for labour increases, and is attracted toward the new investments, with relative wages: this leads in turn encourages demand for consumer goods and prices in this sector also increases. And it is therefore evident that the increase in non-monetary income will not be matched by an increase in real incomes, because of the inflationary effect exerted by unsatisfied demand for consumer goods.

> This increased intensity of the demand for consumers' goods need have no unfavourable effect on investment activity so long as the funds available for investment purposes are sufficiently increased by further credit expansion to claim, in the face of the increasing competition from the consumers' goods industries, such increasing shares of the total

available resources as are required to complete the new processes already under way. (Hayek 1933, 147).

Nevertheless, in order to be sustained, this process requires credit expansion without respite—which would bring about a cumulative increase in prices that sooner or later would exceed every limit. The conflict seems to be evident when demand for consumer goods exceeds the funds available for investment in terms of absolute value. At this point, the interest rate cannot but rise, frustrating demand for capital goods precisely when their price has also risen. A considerable part of the new plant installed, designed to produce other capital goods, remains unused since the further investments required to complete production processes cannot be made (Hayek, 1933, p. 148). As a result, in an advanced stage of the boom, growth in demand for consumer goods brings down demand for higher order goods (Hayek 1939, 31).

> The entrepreneurs who have begun to increase their productive equipment in the expectation that the low rate of interest and the ample supply of money capital would enable them to continue and to utilise these investments under the same favourable conditions, find these *expectations disappointed*. The increase of the prices of all those factors of production that can be used also in the late stages of production will raise the costs of, and at the same time the rise in the rate of interest will decrease the demand for, the capital goods which they produce. And a considerable part of the newly created equipment designed to produce other capital goods will stand idle because the expected further investment in these other capital goods does not materialise.
> This phenomenon of a *scarcity of capital* making it impossible to use the existing capital equipment appears to me the central point of the true explanation of crises. (Hayek 1933, 148–149, my italics).

In this way, Hayek came to the centrality of the *scarcity of capital*, just like Spiethoff,[7] judging it to be "the central point of the true explanation of

---

[7] Hayek (1929, 41n) recognized the close relationship between his own approach and Spiethoff's. And he judged that bond to be even more significant than the one that can exist between different theories of a monetary character. In fact, as emphasised by Steele (2001, 146–147), the central point of Hayekian analysis is the distortion of the production structure rather than the manipulation of the rate of interest. Monetary expansion is merely the trigger, one of the possible aspects that can set off the cyclic mechanism precisely because it is able to modify the structure of capital. Hayek wrote: "Since the publication of the German edition of this book, I have become less convinced that the difference between monetary and non-monetary explanations is the most important point of disagreement

crises" (Hayek 1933, 149). Hayek over the years became so convinced of the centrality of this point that he went as far as to say that "the turn of affairs will be brought about in the end by a "scarcity of capital" independently of whether the money rate of interest rises or not" (Hayek 1939, 32). As we have seen, such a situation can may actually occur even without monetary manipulation but as a result of growing profit expectations which, since the monetary rate is not allowed to rebalance itself with the natural level, cannot find counterparts in realignment with the value of the savings.[8]

If the rate of interest were allowed to rise as profits rise [...], the industries that could not earn profit at this higher rate would have to curtail or stop production [...]. If [...] the rate of interest is kept at the initial low figure [...] and investments whose yield is not negatively affected continue in spite of the rise in final demand, the rise of profits in the late stages of production and the rise of costs will both come into play and will produce the result which the rate of interest has failed to bring about. The rise of the rate of profit on short as compared with that on long investments will induce entrepreneurs to divert whatever funds they have to invest toward less capitalistic machinery, etc.; and whatever part of the required reduction in total investment is not brought about by this diversion of investment demand toward less capitalistic type of machinery will in the end be brought about by a rise in the cost of production of investment goods in the early stages. (Hayek 1939, 32–33).

---

between the various Trade Cycle theories. On the one hand, it seems to me that within the monetary group of explanations the difference between those theorists who regard the superficial phenomena of changes in the value of money as decisive factors in determining cyclical fluctuations, and those who lay emphasis on the real changes in the structure of production brought about by monetary causes, is much greater than the difference between the latter group and such so-called non-monetary theorists as Prof. Spiethoff and Prof. Cassel. On the other hand, it seems to me that the difference between these explanations, which seek the cause of the crisis in the scarcity of capital, and the so-called 'under-consumption' theories, is theoretically as well as practically of much more far-reaching importance than the difference between monetary and non-monetary theories."

[8] Hayek (1929, 81–82) acknowledged Spiethoff's central role in developing a theory of fluctuations founded on disproportionalities and the scarcity of capital but he criticises his German colleague for not identifying the prime reasons for these phenomena. "Assuming that the rate of interest always determines the point to which the available volume of savings enables productive plant to be extended – and is it only by this assumption that we can explain what determines the rate of interest at all – any allegations of a discrepancy between saving and investments must be backed up by a demonstration why, in the given case, interest does not fulfil this function. Professor Spiethoff, like most of the theorists of this group, evades this necessary issue." See also Hayek (1929, 89–90).

Thanks to this analysis, Hayek clarified that (1) the scarcity of capital leads to partial non-use of existing capital goods, (2) the abundance of capital goods is the symptom of a scarcity of capital, and (3) this is not caused by insufficient demand for consumer goods but by excessive demand for these goods. In fact, demand for consumer goods becomes so pressing as to impede any prolonged production process, despite the fact that related means of production are available[9].

Hayek (1931, 67) explained these situations through a straightforward metaphor:

> The situation would be similar to that of a people of an isolated island, if, after having partially constructed an enormous machine which was to provide them with all necessities, they found out that they had exhausted all their savings and available free capital before the new machine could turn out its product. They would then have no choice but to abandon temporarily the work on the new process and to devote all their labour to producing their daily food without any capital. Only after they had put themselves in a position in which new supplies of food were available could they proceed to attempt to get the new machinery into operation.[10]

As we have seen, such a situation can actually occur even without monetary manipulation but as a result of growing profit expectations which, since the monetary rate is not allowed to rebalance itself with the natural level, cannot find counterparts in realignment with the value of the savings.

Thus, the economy is unable to sustain production oriented over and above its capabilities. Sooner or later, it is realized that an increase in wages is cancelled by growing inflation. In addition, capital goods run out, taking with them the over-production in a particular sector and it is here that problems arise. Many economic initiatives set up through excessive reliance on credit cannot be completed, although the debts still have to be paid. Many companies have to be expelled from the system. Capital is scarce, and banks raise interest rates. A period of adjustment and return to equilibrium begins, which may seem abnormal because it has aspects of a crisis.

---

[9] Kurz (2003, 192).
[10] See also Steele (2001, 145).

4.2. From the Sustainable Boom to the *Natural Cycle*

According to the traditional version of the ABCT, economic development would be sustainable if, in typical situations of bright expectations, players were free to learn through interaction with each other and allow their choices to be judged in the market. Without the interference of a monetary rate, players would be forced to determine, in the market, to what extent their expectations are in line with those of other agents, and therefore we would see a growing mutual consistency between different actors' plans. The natural rate, although its magnitude is unknown, is dynamically decided by time preferences, thereby generating a production structure consistent with such preferences. The system would move and settle continuously. In this way, every change in the structure of production would be the adaptation to a change in time preferences, a dynamic adaptation: If profit expectations rise, pushing the natural rate upward, the new production structure could not begin to change until the new natural rate also convinces consumers to change their attitude; at the same time, it is likely that not all the intense demand for new investments would be "met" by new savings, so that the natural rate would tend to stabilize at a lower point than the initial expansionist impetus generated by entrepreneurial expectations. Demand and supply mechanisms will generate, through information transmission, the new price able to link the expectations of investors and consumers.

In a system where there is no central bank, there is no monetary interest rate imposed by central authorities. In such as system, in which an effective free market would operate, there would simply be the natural rate, measuring the structure of time preferences. This means that price system as information transmission mechanism could actually work. What happens in the event of a unilateral modification of time preferences, such as an increase in the savings rate? This is the situation in which consumers become more future-oriented. It is thereby evident that a conflict arises between the time preferences of consumers and those of investors. Yet this also means that the equilibrium rate moves downward, in an attempt also to orient the plans of entrepreneurs toward the future, who would therefore be encouraged to change the structure of the production process, starting with more time-consuming production processes: the new lower interest rate is "informing" investors that new resources are available for long-term investments. These investments will be financed specifically with the new savings. The new equilibrium rate, the only signal for players in the market, allows entrepreneurs to modify their expectations and plans; it informs them that new resources are available and that investments can be implemented profitably. The entrepreneurial instinct, typically Schumpeterian and also emphasized by Spiethoff, thereby allows the re-adaptation of expectations in order to harmonize time preferences.

Consequently, without the interference of the central bank, the natural equilibrium rate (a price generated by the interaction of supply and demand and not imposed by central banks) allows the production structure to adapt to the new system of time preferences. Entrepreneurs' profit expectations, encouraged by the lower rate of interest, are not frustrated because they find a counterpart in the different attitude among consumers, who are now less oriented toward immediate consumption. In this case, the expansion cycle is sustainable because the free interaction of players does not encounter interference and plans can be adapted. This does not mean that, in the process of adaptation, errors are not encountered or that certain expectations will not be frustrated. Preference adaptation is a process that takes place in *real* time, not instantly. However, conditions exist whereby free transmission of information helps one to learn from mistakes and rearrange plans in line with the new situation. And the scenario itself will be continually changing. The re-adaptation process does not take place "once and for all"; it is a continuous and never-tamed process. Nonetheless, it can be implemented in a balanced manner only if the natural rate, is generated by the demand-supply interaction, which is the only signal (price) for the players, assuming divergent signals are not introduced from the outside which may wrongly guide decisions and make the discoordination of preferences perpetual, thereby preventing the free inter-temporal coordination mechanism of plans.

In short, a growth path is generated when time preferences change on a global scale. And this is only possible, according to the Austrian theory, if the central element measuring time preferences—the interest rate—is free to set itself on the market through the interaction of individuals freely exerting their entrepreneurial function in the process of meeting their needs.

In all the cases analyzed so far, we could notice how the boom is always generated by movement toward the future of the intertemporal structure of the preferences. Changing expectations can occur from the consumer side or from the entrepreneur side. What matters is that the result is a lengthening of the structure of production: More roundabout production processes are started by entrepreneurs. These new investments are what are called innovations in the Schumpeterian approach; they generate *development* (Lachmann 1940, 271), or the "spontaneous and discontinuous changes in the channel of the circular flow and [the] disturbances of the centre of equilibrium" (Schumpeter 1934, 65).

It is time to implant some Schumpeterian elements into the theory I sketched so far. This will help us to understand why economic crises are unavoidable. Let us assume that we started from a situation of perfect static equilibrium in which assumptions of perfect competition, constant population, lack of savings, and everything needed to meet the requirements of the circular flow hold true. (Schumpeter 1964, 132–133) (Schumpeter 1964, 29–38 called such a situation of equilibrium the "theoretical standard") It is also assumed that, in the capitalist society model, there will always be the possibility of new combinations and people capable and willing to implement them. (Their motivation is the prospect of profit.)

> [. . .] Some people, then, conceive and work out with varying promptness plans for innovations associated with varying anticipations of profits, and set about struggling with the obstacles incident to doing a new and unfamiliar thing […] we suppose that he founds a new firm, constructs a new plant, and orders new equipment from existing firms. The requisite funds he borrows from a bank. On the balance acquired by so doing he draws, either in order to hand the checks to other people who furnish him with goods and services, or in order to get currency with which to pay for these supplies. […] he withdraws, by his bids for producers' goods, the quantities of them he needs from the uses which they served before.
>
> Then other entrepreneurs follow, after them still others in increasing number, in the path of innovation, which becomes progressively smoothed for successors by accumulating experience and vanishing obstacles. (Schumpeter 1964, 133–134).

What can we observe from the foregoing excerpt? First, Schumpeter assumed that entrepreneurs immediately spend their earnings, except for a minimum reserve. Secondly, since there are no unused resources at the outset (given the circular flow hypothesis), the prices of production factors will increase, along with monetary incomes and the interest rate. Thirdly, revenue will also increase in line with the expenditure by entrepreneurs in investment goods, as will incomes of workers, temporarily employed with higher wages, and those of everyone receiving all those higher payments (Schumpeter 1964, 134). However, up to this point, it is legitimate to assume that there has not yet been an increase in production (Schumpeter 1964, 135). This is what happens until the plant of the first entrepreneur begins to operate (Schumpeter 1964, 136).

[. . .] Then the scene begins to change. The new commodities—let us say, new consumers' goods—flow into the market. They are, since everything turns out according to expectation, readily taken up at exactly those prices at which the entrepreneur expected to sell them. [...] A stream of receipts will hence flow into the entrepreneur's account, at a rate sufficient to repay, during the lifetime of the plant and equipment originally acquired, the total debt incurred plus interest, and to leave a profit for the entrepreneur. [...] the new firms, getting successively into working order and throwing their products into the market of consumers' goods, increase the total output of consumers' goods [...]. (Schumpeter 1964, 136).

The new goods, according to Schumpeter, enter the market too quickly to be absorbed smoothly. In particular, the old enterprises and the pursuers have several possible scenarios before them, but there is no fixed rule: some become part of the new scenario, others close because they are unable to adapt, others still seek rationalization (Schumpeter 1964, 137–138). However, the competitive advantage of the driving company tends to fade, since, as the new products progressively come on to the market and the debt repayments quantitatively increase in importance, entrepreneurial activity tends to diminish to the point of disappearing altogether (Schumpeter 1964, 138). As soon as entrepreneurial impetus loses steam, pulling the system away from its previous area of equilibrium, the system embarks on a struggle toward a new equilibrium. The initial outline of a cyclic pattern can be seen (Schumpeter 1964, 142).

[. . .] Each of those two phases is characterized by a definite succession of phenomena. The reader need only recall what they are in order to make the discovery that they are precisely the phenomenon which he associates with "prosperity" and "recession": our model reproduces, by its mere working, that very sequence of events which we observe in the course of those fluctuations in economic life which have come to be called business cycles and which, translated into the language of diagrams, present the picture of an undulating or wavelike movement in absolute figures or rates of change. (Schumpeter 1964, 142).

The following is the reasoning that leads to the second approximation of the cycle. If innovations are incorporated into new plant and equipment, spending on consumer goods will increase at least as fast as spending on capital goods. Both will expand starting from those points in the system where they exerted the first impact and will create that set of economic situations which we call prosperity. Two phenomena arise here: First, old businesses will react to this situation; and, second, a number of them *will speculate on it.* Those who seek to take advantage of the situation by speculating, act on the assumption that the rates of change they observe will continue indefinitely. Such an attitude anticipates prosperity, causing a *boom* (Schumpeter 1964, 150). At this point, transactions join the picture that, in order to become possible, assume an expected or effective increase in prices. This is how, in the cyclic process, a secondary wave comes into play, the effects of which overlap those of the primary wave (Schumpeter 1964, 151). The outcomes of the new wave are also more visible than the first wave.

Even in secondary prosperity, the break is induced by a turning point in the underlying process. Any state of prosperity, however ideally limited to essential primary processes, involves a period of failures that, in addition to eliminating enterprises that are obsolete beyond any chance of re-adaptation, also gives rise to a painful process of readjustment ofprices, quantities, and values as the framework of a new system of equilibrium progressively emerges (Schumpeter 1964, 153–154). Secondary prosperity even sees risky, fraudulent, or, in any case, unlucky initiatives take shape that are unable to cope with the recession (entrepreneurs defined as imitators and speculators who simply follow the situation of change). The speculative position involves many unsustainable elements, which even a minimal deterioration of the value of collateral elements will cause a fall. As a result, a great deal of the day-to-day business and investments will suffer a loss as soon as prices fall, as they undoubtedly will in view of the primary process. A portion of the debt structure will also collapse. If panic and crisis prevail under these conditions, further adjustments become necessary: Values fall, and every fall brings with it yet another fall. For a certain time, the pessimistic expectation may play a decisive role, even if it subsequently does not hold up unless substantiated by objective factors (Schumpeter 1964, 154). A cyclical pattern with four stages is consequently outlined (Remember that first approximation only included prosperity and recession): prosperity, recession, depression, and recovery.

For our purposes, it is vital to emphasize the characteristic element of secondary prosperity: imitations and their role in further swelling the growth process. As acknowledged by Lachmann (1986, 15), a "competitive process taking place within the market for a good consists typically of two phases, and in it the factors of innovation and imitation may be isolated as iterative elements."[11] The expansion stage of the cycle is always characterized by the time expansion of the production structure—an expansion that occurs because of investments usually associated with that sector of assets linked to growing profit expectations and in turn stimulated by a certain kind of credit policy or change in time preferences. The success of the first investments, when the liquidation process is not yet on the horizon, modifies information, and the expectations of many other subjects contribute toward intensifying the magnitude of expansion, because they attract imitators who make additional investments, usually financed by credit,.

Following the introduction of Schumpeterian imitation/speculation processes and the Lachmannian accent on expectations, I shall attempt to demonstrate how crisis is a consequence of all stages of growth and how sustainable and artificial booms are not distinguished by the onset of a depression but by its intensity and duration. Consequently, in my view, the growth stage will be followed by a process of resettlement (crisis) even in the case of a "healthy" expansion. This is because—even for sustainable development—positive profit expectations facilitate the appearance of speculative-imitative initiatives once the cycle has been set in motion that must be liquidated at a given point in order to "normalize" the progress of growth. What distinguishes sustainable development from an artificial boom is not the emergence of a crisis; the difference lies in the *nature* of the crisis and its *intensity*.

The crucial elements in my analysis, therefore, are expectations and the imitative process. As we have seen, Hayek (1929, 147) recognized the central role of expectations as early as 1929, when he emphasized profit expectations as the driving force behind entrepreneurial preferences, with the possibility of entrepreneurs becoming more future-oriented and thus shifting the equilibrium interest rate upward. Profit expectations are a key element in both the Hayekian vision of sustainable growth and in the opposite case. I will use them to describe the emergence of imitations and secondary expansion, then followed by a crisis. It is now time to see how the so-called *sustainable growth* in Austrian theory turned, in our view, into the *natural cycle* (Ferlito 2014).

In the ideal situation where the monetary rate does not exist (nor the central bank), time-intensive investment processes emerge when either consumers or investors become more future-oriented. If consumers are the first to change their preferences, this will take the form of growing savings followed by a decrease in the natural rate of interest, in order to attract

---

[11] See also Lewin (1997, 15).

investors to use those resources for more roundabout investments. If, on the other hand, entrepreneurs are the first to push toward lengthening of the production structure, the natural rate will rise in order to attract savers in the same direction, thereby providing necessary resources for new investments. In both cases, the natural rate is driven by a change in the structure of temporal preferences, in turn generated by different expectations. What follows is a process of sustainable development.

The role of business expectations in generating longer investment projects is also emphasized by Schumpeter. We have seen earlier how Hayek referred explicitly to Schumpeter in highlighting the innovative and investment process that follows positive profit expectations. In this process of expansion, in accordance with the traditional version of the ABCT, the aspects needed to generate a crisis do not arise.

However, observation of reality leads to emphasize, following Schumpeter and Lachmann, that the first wave of investments it is always followed by a secondary wave of imitations and speculations. As analyzed above, the pace of economic growth becomes particularly sustained when the primary wave of entrepreneurial investments is joined by a stage of secondary growth encouraged by the instincts of imitators in search of profit and driven by "fashion." Why are imitations inevitable? This is what we have already seen as regards Lachmann's vision of capitalist development characterized by innovation and imitation. Keeping faith with subjectivism and the role of expectations, it is easy to imagine how the success of entrepreneurial initiatives is readily followed by imitators looking for success within which a period of growth destined never to end always seems to exist at first sight. The primary stage of growth is characterized by investment set in motion by a limited number of entrepreneurs—those who are able to seize opportunities that go unnoticed by most people and are therefore the first to change their expectations (Schumpeterian entrepreneurs). The secondary stage is characterized by the appearance on the market of an exceptional number of imitators, driven by profit expectations arising from observing the onset of the boom initiated by the first innovative entrepreneurs.

This is how I identify the first two stages in our natural cycle: primary expansion, generated by a change in the structure of time preferences and expectations (the system becomes more future-oriented), and secondary expansion characterized by imitative investments.

If, therefore, the reality of imitative speculation cannot be eliminated, it outlines the character of the growth process by emphasizing development above the initially imagined level. Like the primary wave of investments, the second wave is generated by profit expectations, particularly the expectation that the current situation will not change (Schumpeter 1939, 145). From a quantitative point of view, moreover, imitation (secondary) investment might even be greater than the first cycle of investment since it involves a larger number of individuals, whose expectations are "overexcited" by the boom (Schumpeter 1939, 146). These secondary investments will have to be liquidated through an adjustment crisis, as I shall attempt to demonstrate.

The fact that secondary wave investments necessarily bring about their liquidation, by generating a crisis, even for booms not induced artificially by discoordination between natural and monetary rates, apparently seems to be at odds with the traditional version of the Austrian theory, which does not admit crises whenever such discoordination is not at the base of the growth process. I believe, on the other hand, that—while not denying the validity of the Austrian approach—this vision should be replaced.

Let us summarize the appearance of primary expansion characterizing our natural cycle. When, given positive profit expectations, entrepreneurs become more future-oriented, the natural rate of interest rises, in order to move consumer preferences in the same direction, encouraging them to save more and thereby generate resources to meet increased demand for loanable funds by investors. The mirror-image situation arises when consumer expectations change in a more future-oriented direction; In this case, the natural rate of interest falls, informing entrepreneurs that new resources are available for investments in the longer term. Both situations, to use "Austrian" jargon, give rise to a sustainable boom.

According to this schema, current investments will always find available resources to complete the business projects launched given that the lengthening of the production structure derives from a change in time preferences and market operators and are not deceived by a monetary rate inconsistent with the natural rate. This is precisely because, without the interference of political-monetary authorities, market operators are free to "reveal themselves" to each other and readjust their scheme of preferences in conformity with the modified situation.

However, we have the distinct impression that this view does not take a fundamental fact into account: the *rhythm* of investments in *real time*. The Schumpeterian distinction between primary wave and secondary wave investments in this regard becomes critical. In fact, the initial increase in investment followed by a change in the structure of time preferences does not seem to generate any problem. Whether savings grow or the natural interest rate increases because of profit expectations, the timing of the onset of business ventures is necessarily dictated by the realignment of preferences. In fact, when savings increase the problem does not arise precisely because the increased resources are the first cause of the reduction of the natural rate and the lengthening of the productive structure its consequence. All the more, if there is increased demand for loanable funds, new resources for investment will not be available until consumers decide to increase their propensity to save; that is, until the intentions of the two groups of players re-align again.

The matter changes when a second wave of investment generated by the imitative process comes into play. It is first and foremost a natural fact, intrinsic to a boom, regardless of its type. Indeed, as Schumpeter emphasized, innovation is never generated as a mass phenomenon; on the contrary, it arises through the initiative of certain "elect spirits"—entrepreneurs—whose essence lies precisely in being able to grasp profit opportunities where others fail to see them. In any case, when the expansion phenomenon is subsequently set in motion—when an opportunity for profit has already been identified and grasped by some people—the prospect of grabbing a slice of the cake becomes tempting for many (the role of expectations). This is not a temptation for those who have seized the opportunity and, having begun to invest, are now on the way toward reaping their reward but for those who were bystanders and are now seeking to take part in the boom stage (with a time lapse compared to the primary wave).

What form does the imitative desire take? It generates new demand for loanable funds in order to insert a more roundabout production process into the expansive cycle. This means an attempt to extend the expansion process temporarily, thereby also increasing the degree of uncertainty.

More time taken implies more things can happen—providing the possibility of greater productivity but also greater uncertainty. Since the value of a higher order (capital) good depends on the prospective value of the consumer goods it is expected to produce, the elapse of time and with it the arrival of unexpected events, implies that some production plans are bound to be disappointed, and thus the value of specific capital goods will be affected. (Lewin 2005, 151).

And this brings us to the second stage of the natural cycle: secondary expansion. Pressure on demand for loanable funds forces the natural interest rate to rise further in order to attract new savings to finance these investments. And this is where the role of banks joins the game to a very similar degree as that described by Schumpeter. Initially, demand for loanable funds cannot be met because preferences have not yet realigned with the new interest rate level, and it is even likely that such a realignment does not actually take place.

However, the positive sentiment, positive profit expectations, that becomes "incandescent" at the end of the primary expansion stage also plays a role as regards the action of banks. In fact, precisely because of what happens during expansion, it is highly likely that banks make available "virtual funds" that are not backed up by real savings (as is the case during the first wave of investments), driven by expectations, because of the enthusiasm generated by the boom.

On the other hand, it is more than likely that the long-awaited realignment does not come about. Even though the natural rate may increase, in view of the profit expectations arising from the request for a second wave of investment. (imitative), the likelihood that savings may increase is limited by two factors. The most obvious one, of course, is that consumers must also consume; hence their capacity for saving (and realignment) is objectively limited by the necessity to consume. In addition, in all likelihood, consumers will also be influenced by the general enthusiasm of the boom stage and consequently change their preferences in the opposite direction, i.e., change by increasing their propensity for consumption. This is all the more true given the fact that real wages grow during the boom in order to attract workers into the new investment areas or to employ formerly unemployed workers. As in the conventional Austrian explanation, this leads to pressure in demand for consumer goods, with an initial phenomenon of forced savings and the production structure subsequent need to return to present-oriented projects (consumer goods). At this point, the growth of price and wages and the pressure on prices goods of consumer goods brings about what Hayek called the "Ricardo effect": it helps explain why a prolonged boom stage driven by monetary expansion is likely to turn into a crisis:

> [. . .] [I]f the credit expansion boom does not come to an end sooner for some other reason, it must come to an end when consumer product prices advance ahead of wage and resource prices. The Ricardo effect lowers real wages and encourages a shift toward labor-intensive methods of production. A lowering of the real wage of labor makes short-term (labor-intensive) projects appear to be more profitable than long-term (capital-intensive) methods of production. The Ricardo effect may account for the sudden wave of bankruptcies among the large fixed-investment projects that occurred toward the end of many nineteenth-century business cycles. (Moss 2005, 8–9).

So, while the first wave of investments can complete its cycle because of the real existence of prior and stable funds (without which the expansion cycle would not even have started), the second wave will be frustrated by a change in consumer preferences and a banking policy influenced by profit expectations.

The difference between sustainable growth and artificial boom, therefore, lies in the following fact: When the "defective" cycle is triggered by a discoordination between a natural rate and a monetary rate controlled by the monetary authorities, it is generally true that many of the roundabout processes of production end up being frustrated by the onset of the Hayekian phenomenon of scarcity of capital as described above. On the other hand, in the case of a sustainable boom (*natural cycle*) generated by a change in expectations, a crisis will be the necessary action to liquidate faulty initiatives only because of the inevitable wave of speculative-imitative investment, backed up by a banking policy influenced by a positive sentiment, which itself will later be frustrated.

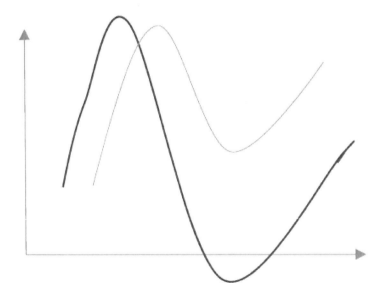

Figure 2. Monetary Cycle vs. Natural Cycle.

What will follow in the latter case will be a crisis (third stage of the natural cycle) but one that is limited in terms of intensity, duration, and the number of sectors involved. We could even define it as a transitory readjustment crisis that does not eliminate the beneficial effects of the previous boom but merely liquidates business ventures launched for speculative-imitative purposes. What will not follow is a fourth stage, a depression, which is typical of the unsustainable cycle. Figure 2 graphically shows the differences between the monetary cycle and the natural cycle.

5. CAPITAL AND BUSINESS CYCLES

Is there any relationship between the business cycles as we just described them and capital as defined in Chapter 1? Yes, capital formation and business cycles are related by the fact that both phenomena are arising in the process of expectations formation. Indeed, the typical manifestation of the different stages of the business cycle consists in capital modifications: They are the micro-elements at the very root of economic fluctuations.

We saw that the first expansion phase of a cycle begins with rising profit expectations, a phenomenon that can be due to many factors, including simply an apparently irrational, positive mood. In particular, an expansionary stage is often related to one particular good or to a particular group of goods. I do not necessarily have in mind Schumpeterian innovations. If the 2000–2001 boom and bust cycle related to the so called *new economy* was linked with typically Schumpeterian new combinations, the more recent the 2004–2006 expansion was pulled by the property industry, a traditional one. We can therefore say that a boom arises when profit expectations focus on a particular industry that will pull the general economic system into the cyclical process. The hermeneutical moment involving capital at this stage is such that we observe a high number of capital goods combinations implemented in production processes inside the driving industry. What happens to capital, therefore, is to be determined by the combination of goods which are thought to be suitable to producing something related to the pulling industry.

During the first stage of the boom, such a concentration of capital combinations inside a certain industry may appear quantitatively limited, in particular if it is related to a Schumpeterian innovation, one that is brought out at the beginning only be few pioneers. The phenomenon becomes more clearly evident during the second stage of the boom when the amount of imitative and speculation processes sum up to the initial investment wave.

Instead what will happen, during the crisis and depression stages is a typical process of capital destruction (what Hayek and Spiethoff called "scarcity of capital"). For the reasons described when I talked about the monetary and the natural cycles, many projects will have to be abandoned because they are no longer profitable or because of a shift toward the production of goods closer to the final stage of consumption. I refer to capital destruction *stricto sensu*, keeping valid the capital definitions outlined in Chapter 1. In fact, even if the goods used in the production processes are not physically destroyed, their combination loses its meaning. As we saw in Chapter 1, certain goods become capital only because, in combination with others, they can generate production processes able to fulfill expectations. Economic actors will have to go through a complicated process of capital re-shaping, involving a totally new hermeneutical process related to the situation arising from the new economic environment. Certain goods have to be thought of in combination with other goods, in different production processes. Certain other goods cannot be utilized at all.

It makes sense to talk about capital destruction during crises and depressions because *specific* production processes are abandoned. Having defined *capital* as a combination of goods implemented for fulfilling expectations, what happens to capital as that specific combination disappears in the face of changing expectations that require new goods combinations? The capital, so intended, is actually destroyed, because its place as part of a certain combination has lost its *raison d'être*, its defining *meaning*.

In short, from the perspective of capital theory, business cycles can be seen as the alternating processes of capital creation and capital destruction. To fulfill rising profit expectations, which are often identified with the production of a specific good or related with a certain industry, goods combination are finalistically implemented; capital is indeed created. With the emergence of a different scenario and the change of expectations which mark the arrival of a crisis, capital is destroyed; some of the combinations implemented with the specific task to produce the cycle-pulling could lose its value. A process of capital destruction arises.

What distinguish the monetary cycle from the natural one is the intensity of capital destruction. In the first case, due to the artificial nature of the expansionary stage, most of the capital creation processes that emerged during the two expansionary stages will be liquidated in the two phases which I called "crisis" and "depression." In case of the natural cycle, we face capital destruction to a lesser extent instead, and it is mainly the capital creation that occurred during the secondary boom that will face a liquidation, while processes initiated during the first stage of the boom will not encounter the same fate because of the context in which they arose (sustainable boom).

CONCLUSION

The analysis developed so far allows us to conclude, in a very simple way and in the wake of authoritative economists of the past, that the cyclical trend is the form that development takes in a capitalist economy.

While acknowledging the basic assumptions of the Austrian Business Cycle Theory as valid, especially in Hayek's version, the systematic introduction of "real" expectations, acting in "real time," in the sense advocated by Ludwig Lachmann, can only lead us toward the rediscovery of secondary investment waves (imitations and speculations) on which Schumpeter focused in particular. By being enabled by a banking policy sensitive to, and part of, the generally positive sentiment of an expansion stage, they precisely match that part of the growth stage that has to be liquidated through a readjustment crisis.

I therefore believe that the Austrian distinction between sustainable and unsustainable growth is valid. What I rather seek to overcome is the belief that, in the first case, the expansion stage is not followed by a crisis. On the contrary, a liquidation crisis occurs in both cases. The difference lies in the intensity and duration of the crisis. Most of the long-term entrepreneurial projects initiated by entrepreneurs will struggle to achieve completion in the case of a boom generated from the outset in an "unhealthy" manner. For growth set in motion in a "sustainable" manner, only the imitative and speculative initiatives will not be completed. As a result, the positive effects of the first part of the expansion will not be eliminated. It is merely a question of "clearing up." I call this instance the *natural cycle*. In the previous case, on the other hand, reconstruction will have to begin from a pile of rubble.

The same happens with capital. While in the case of what I called the "monetary cycle" most of the capital creation that occurred during the boom will face destruction (loss of meaning), in the case of a natural cycle only certain combinations, those that emerged during the secondary boom, will encounter the destructive fate.

REFERENCES

Antiseri, Dario. (2011). *Contro Rothbard. Elogio dell'ermeneutica.* Soviera Mannelli: Rubbettino.

Bellet, Michel, and Jacques Durieu. (2004). "Lundberg and Lachmann on expectations." In *Evolution of the market process: Austrian and Swedish economics*, edited by Michel Bellet, Sandye Gloria-Palermo, and Abdallah Zouache, 230–252. London and New York: Routledge.

Blundell, John. (2014). "IHS and the rebirth of Austrian economics: Some reflections on 1974–1976." *The Quarterly Journal of Austrian Economics* 17(1):92–107. Retrieved from *https://mises.org/library/ihs-and-rebirth-austrian-economics-some-reflections-1974–1976*.

Becker, Marcus C., Thorbjørn Knudsen, and Richard Swedberg. (2011a). "Introduction." In *The Entrepreneur: Classic Texts by Joseph Schumpeter*, by Joseph Schumpeter, 1–42. Stanford: Stanford University Press.

Becker, Marcus C., Thorbjørn Knudsen, and Richard Swedberg, eds. (2011b). *The Entrepreneur: Classic Texts by Joseph Schumpeter.* Stanford: Stanford University Press.

Boettke, Peter J., Steven Horwitz, and David L. Prychitko. (1986). "Beyond equilibrium economics: Reflections on the uniqueness of the austrian tradition." In *Modern Austrian Economics. Archaeology of a Revival*, Volume 2, *The age of dispersal*, edited by Sandy Gloria-Palermo, 121–132. London: Pickering and Chatto, 2002.

Böhm-Bawerk, Eugen von. (1884). *Capital and interest. A critical history of economical theory.* London and New York: Macmillan and Co., 1890.

Böhm-Bawerk, Eugen von. (1889). *The positive theory of capital.* New York: G.E. Stechert, 1930.

Braudel, Fernand. (1979). *Civilization & capitalism. 15th-18th century*, Volume 2, *The Wheels of Commerce*. Berkeley and Los Angeles: University of California Press, 1992.

Cowan, Ronin, and Mario J. Rizzo. (1996). "The genetic-causal tradition and modern economic theory." In *Modern Austrian Economics: Archaeology of a Revival*, Volume 1, *A multi-directional revival*, edited by Sandye Gloria-Palermo, 315–360. London: Pickering & Chatto, 2002.

Di Iorio, Francesco. (2015a). *Cognitive autonomy and methodological. individualism: The interpretative foundations of social life*. New York: Springer Publishing.

Di Iorio, Francesco. (2015b). "Hayek and the hermeneutics of mind." *Social Science Information* 54(2):177–191.

Di Nuoscio, Enzo. (2014). *Ermeneutica ed economia. Spiegazione ed interpretazione dei fatti economici*. Soveria Mannelli: Rubbettino.

Ebner, Alexander. (2006). "Schumpeterian entrepreneurship revisited: Historical specificity and the phases of capitalist development." *Journal of the History of Economic Thought* 28(3):315–332.

Evola, Julius. (1931). "Universalità imperiale e particolarismo nazionalistico." In *Il federalismo imperiale. Scritti sull'idea di Impero 1926-1953*, edited by Giovanni Perez, 81–92. Rome and Naples: Fondazione Julius Evola and Controcorrente, 2004.

Evola, Julius. (1942). "L'Impero e la cultura europea." In *Il federalismo imperiale. Scritti sull'idea di impero 1926-1953*, edited by Giovanni Perez, 135–150. Rome and Naples: Fondazione Julius Evola and Controcorrente, 2004.

Fanno, Marco. (1931). "Production cycles, credit cycles, and industrial fluctuations." In *Business Cycle Theory. Selected Texts 1860-1939*, Volume 2, *Structural theories of the business cycle*, edited by Harald Hagemann, 225–261. London: Pickering and Chatto, 2002.

Ferlito, Carmelo. (2011). "Sylos Labini's unpublished notes on Schumpeter's Business Cycles." *The Quarterly Journal of Austrian Economics*, 14(1):88–129. Retreived from *https://mises.org/library/sylos-labinis-unpublished-notes-schumpeters-business-cycles*.

Ferlito, Carmelo. (2013). *Phoenix Economics: From Crisis to Renascence*. Hauppague: Nova Publishers.

Ferlito, Carmelo. (2014). "The natural cycle: Why economic fluctuations are inevitable. A Schumpeterian extension of the Austrian business cycle theory." *Journal of Reviews on Global Economics*, 3:200–219. DOI: http://dx.doi.org/10.6000/1929-7092.2014.03.16.

Ferlito, Carmelo. (2015a). "Entrepreneurship: State of grace or human action? Schumpeter's leadership vs Kirzner's alertness." *European Journal of Economic and Social Systems*, 27(1-2):11–36.

Ferlito, Carmelo, ed. (2015b). "Editorial: Hayek, Keynes and the crisis: Analyses and remedies." *Journal of Reviews on Global Economics*, 4:184–280.

Ferlito, Carmelo. (2015c). "At the root of economic fluctuations: Expectations, preferences and innovation. Theoretical framework and empirical evidences." Paper presented at the World Economics Association (WEA) Conference No. 2, The European Crisis, October 1–December 1.

Ferlito, Carmelo. (2015d). "Disproportionality and business cycle from Tugan-Baranovskij to Spiethoff." *Journal of Reviews on Global Economics*, 4:108–119. DOI: http://dx.doi.org/10.6000/1929-7092.2015.04.10.

Fetter, Frank. (1977). *Capital, interest, and rent*. Kansas City: Sheed Andrews and McMeel, Inc.

Foss, Nicolai J. (2012). "The continuing relevance of Austrian capital theory." *The Quarterly Journal of Austrian Economics*, 15(2):151–171. Retrieved from *https://mises.org/library/continuing-relevance-austrian-capital-theory-0*.

Garrison, Roger W. (1986). "From Lachmann to Lucas: On institutions, expectations, and equilibrating tendencies." In *Subjectivism, intelligibility, and economic understanding: Essays in honor of Ludwig M. Lachmann on his eightieth birthday*, edited by Israel M. Kirzner, 87–101. New York and London: New York University Press and Macmillan and Co.

Garrison, Roger W. (2001). *Time and money: The macroeconomics of capital structure*. London and New York: Routledge.

Garrison, Roger W. (2006). "The Natural rate of interest in theory and policy formulation." *The Quarterly Journal of Austrian Economics*, 9(4):57–68. Retrieved from *https://mises.org/library/natural-and-neutral-rates-interest-theory-and-policy-formulation*.

Gloria-Palermo, Sandye, and Giulio Palermo. (2004). "To what extent is the Austrian theory of capital Austrian? Böhm-Bawerk and Hicks reconsidered." In *Evolution of the market process: Austrian and Swedish economics*, edited by Michel Bellet, Sandye Gloria-Palermo, and Abdallah Zouache, pp. 197–210. London and New York: Routledge.

Harris, Donald J. (2005). "Robinson on 'history versus equilibrium.'" In *Joan Robinson's economics. A centennial celebration*, edited by Bill Gibson, 81–108. Cheltenham and Northampton: Edward Elgar.

Hayek, Friedrich A. von. (1929). *Monetary theory and the trade cycle*. New York: Kelley, 1966.

Hayek, Friedrich A. von. (1931). *Prices and production*. New York: Augustus M. Kelley, 1967.

Hayek, Friedrich A. von. (1932). "A note on the development of the doctrine of 'forced saving.'" *Quarterly Journal of Economics*, V47:123–133.

Hayek, Friedrich A. von. (1933). "Price expectations, monetary disturbances and malinvestments." In *Profits, interest and investment: and other essays on the theory of industrial fluctuations*, by Friedrich A. von Hayek, 135–156. Clifton: Augustus M. Kelley, 1975.

Hayek, Friedrich A. von. (1934). "Carl Menger." In *Principle of economics*, by Carl Menger, 11–36. Auburn: Ludwig von Mises Institute, 2007.

Hayek, Friedrich A. von. (1939). "Profits, interest and investment." In *Profits, interest and investment: And other essays on the theory of industrial fluctuations*, by Friedrich A. von Hayek, 3–71. New York: Augustus M. Kelley, 1975.

Hayek, Friedrich A. von. (1941). *The pure theory of capital*. Chicago: The University of Chicago Press, 1952.

Hayek, Friedrich A. von. (1967). *Studies in philosophy, politics and economics*. London: Routledge and Kegan Paul.

Hennings, Klaus H. (2007). *The Austrian theory of value and capital. Studies in the life and work of Eugen von Böhm-Bawerk*. Cheltenham and Brookfields: Edward Elgar.

Horwitz, Steven. (2000). *Microfoundations and macroeconomics: An Austrian perspective*. New York: Routledge.

Huerta de Soto, Jesús. (1992). *Socialism, economic calculation and entrepreneurship*. Cheltenham and Northampton: Edward Elgar, 2010.

Huerta de Soto, Jesús. (1998). *Money, bank credit, and economic cycles*. Auburn: Ludwig von Mises Institute, 2006.

Huerta de Soto, Jesús. (2000). *The Austrian school: Market order and entrepreneurial creativity*. Cheltenham and Northampton: Edward Elgar, 2010.

Hülsmann, Jörg G. (2013). *Krise der inflationskultur. Geld, finanzen und staat in zeiten der kollektiven korruption*. Munich: Finanzbuch Verlag.

Kirzner, Israel M. 1960. *The Economic Point of View*. Kansas City: Sheed and Ward, 1976.

Kirzner, Israel M. (1963). *Market theory and the price system*. Princeton, Toronto, New York, and London: D. van Nostrand.

Kirzner, Israel M. (1966). "An essay on capital." In *Essays on capital and interest: An Austrian perspective*, by Israel M. Kirzner, 13–122. Cheltenham: Edward Elgar, 1996.

Kirzner, Israel M. (1973). *Competition and entrepreneurship*. Chicago: University of Chicago Press.

Kirzner, Israel M. (1992). *The Meaning of market process: Essays in the development of modern Austrian economics*. London and New York: Routledge.

Kirzner, Israel M. (1997). "Entrepreneurial discovery and the competitive market process: An Austrian approach." *Journal of Economic Literature*, XXXV:60–85.

Kirzner, Israel M. (1999). "Creativity and/or alertness: A Reconsideration of the Schumpeterian entrepreneur." *Review of Austrian Economics*, 11:5–17.

Kirzner, Israel M. (2000). *The driving force of the market: Essays in Austrian economics*. London and New York: Routledge.

Kirzner, Israel M. (2008). "The alert and creative entrepreneur: A clarification." *IFN working paper no. 760*. Stockholm: Research Institute of Industrial Economics.

Koppl, Roger. (1998). "Lachmann on the subjectivism of active minds." In *Subjectivism and economic analysis: Essays in memory of Ludwig M. Lachmann*, edited by Roger Koppl, and Gary Mongiovi, 61–79. London and New York: Routledge, 2003.

Koppl, Roger. (2014). *From crisis to confidence: Macroeconomics after the Crash*. London: The Institute of Economic Affairs.

Koppl, Roger, and Gary Mongiovi, eds. (1998). *Subjectivism and economic analysis: Essays in memory of Ludwig M. Lachmann*. London and New York: Routledge, 2003.

Kurz, Heinz D. (2003). "Friedrich August Hayek: la teoria monetaria del sovrainvestimento." In *Friedrich A. von Hayek e la Scuola Austriaca di Economia*, edited by Ulrike Ternowetz, 175–207. Rubbettino: Soveria Mannelli.

Lachmann, Ludwig M. (1940). "A reconsideration of the Austrian theory of industrial fluctuations." In *Capital, expectations, and the market process*, edited by Walter E. Grinder, 267–286. Kansas City: Sheed Andrews and McMeel Inc., 1977.

Lachmann, Ludwig M. (1941). "On the measurement of capital." In *Expectations and the meaning of institutions: Essays in economics by*

Ludwig Lachmann, edited by Don Lavoie, 87–101. London and New York: Routledge, 1994.

Lachmann, Ludwig M. (1943). "The role of expectations in economics as a social science." In *Capital, expectations, and the market process*, edited by Walter E. Grinder, 65–80. Kansas City: Sheed Andrews and McMeel Inc., 1977.

Lachmann, Ludwig M. (1947). "Complementarity and substitution in the theory of capital." In *Capital, expectations, and the market process*, edited by Walter E. Grinder, 197–213. Kansas City: Sheed Andrews and McMeel Inc., 1977.

Lachmann, Ludwig M. (1956). *Capital and Its Structure*. Kansas City: Sheed Andrews and McMeel, 1978.

Lachmann, Ludwig M. (1971). *The Legacy of Max Weber*. Berkeley: The Glendessary Press.

Lachmann, Ludwig M. (1973a). *Macro-economic thinking and the market economy: An essay on the neglect of the micro-foundations and its consequences*. London: The Institute of Economic Affairs.

Lachmann, Ludwig M. (1973b). "Sir John Hicks as a neo-Austrian." In *Capital, expectations, and the market process*, edited by Walter E. Grinder, 251–266. Kansas City: Sheed Andrews and McMeel, Inc., 1977.

Lachmann, Ludwig M. (1976a). "Austrian Economics in the present crisis of economic thought." In *Capital, expectations, and the market process*, edited by Walter E. Grinder, 25–41. Kansas City: Sheed Andrews And McMeel Inc., 1977.

Lachmann, Ludwig M. (1976b). "On the central concept of Austrian economics: Market process." In *The foundations of modern Austrian economics*, edited by Edwin G. Dolan, 126–132. Kansas City: Sheed & Ward.

Lachmann, Ludwig M. (1976c). "Toward a critique of macroeconomics." In *The foundations of modern Austrian economics*, edited by Edwin G. Dolan, 152–158. Kansas City: Sheed & Ward.

Lachmann, Ludwig M. (1976d). "From mises to shackle: An essay on Austrian economics and the kaleidic society." *Journal of Economic Literature*, 14(1):54–62.

Lachmann, Ludwig M. (1976e). "On Austrian Capital Theory." In *Modern Austrian economics: Archaeology of a revival*, Volume 1, *A multi-directional revival*, edited by Sandye Gloria-Palermo, 305–313. London: Pickering & Chatto, 2002.

Lachmann, Ludwig M. (1986). *The market as economic process*. Oxford: Basil Blackwell.

Lachmann, Ludwig M. (1990). "Austrian economics: A hermeneutic approach." In *Economics and hermeneutics*, edited by Don Lavoie, 132–144. London and New York: Routledge.

Lavoie, Don, ed. (1990). *Economics and hermeneutics*. London and New York: Routledge.

Leijonhufvud, Axel. (1986). "Capitalism and the factory system." In *Economic as a process: Essays in the new institutional economics*, edited by Richard N. Langlois, 203–223. New York: Cambridge University Press.

Lewin, Peter. (1996). "A Short Course in Capital Theory." In *Modern Austrian Economics. Archaeology of a Revival*, Volume 1, *A Multi-Directional Revival*, edited by Sandye Gloria-Palermo, 277–303. London: Pickering & Chatto, 2002.

Lewin, Peter. (1997). "Capital in disequilibrium: A re-examination of the capital theory of Ludwig M. Lachmann." Unpublished draft. URL: http://www.utdallas.edu/~plewin/hopentrv.pdf.

Lewin, Peter. (2005). "The capital idea and the scope of economics." *The Review of Austrian Economics*, 18(2):145–167.

Lewin, Peter. (2011). *Capital in disequilibrium: The Role of capital in a changing world*. Auburn: Ludwig von Mises Institute.

Meacci, Ferdinando. (2006). "Uncertainty and expectations in shackle's theory of capital and interest." *MPRA paper 11700*. Munich: Munich Personal RePEc Archive. *Retrieved from http://mpra.ub.uni-muenchen.de/11700/*.

Meacci, Ferdinando, and Carmelo Ferlito. (2016). "The classical roots of the Austrian theory of capital." Paper presented at the SIBR-UniKL Conference on Interdisciplinary Business and Economics Research, Kuala Lumpur, February 12-13.

Menegazzi, Guido. (1970). *Il piano dello sviluppo solidale dei popoli*. Milan: Giuffrè.

Menger, Carl. (1871). *Principles of economics*. Auburn: Ludwig von Mises Institute, 2007.

Mises, Ludwig von. (1912). *The theory of money and credit*. Indianapolis: Liberty Fund, 1980.

Mises, Ludwig von. (1936). "The 'Austrian' Theory of the Trade Cycle." In *The Austrian Theory of the Trade Cycle and Other Essays*, edited by Richard M. Ebeling, 25–35. Auburn: Ludwig von Mises Institute, 1980.

Mises, Ludwig von. (1949). *Human action: A treatise on economics*. Auburn: Ludwig von Mises Institute, 1998.

Mises, Ludwig von. (2011). "Human action: The rate of interest." In *The pure-time preference theory of interest*, edited by Jeffrey M. Herbener, 67–84. Auburn: Ludwig von Mises Institute.

Mittermaier, Karl H.M. (1992). "Ludwig Lachmann (1906-1990): A biographical sketch." In *Modern austrian economics. Archaeology of a revival*, Volume 1, *A multi-directional revival*, edited by Sandye Gloria-Palermo, 252–269. London: Pickering & Chatto, 2002.

Moss, Laurence S., ed. 2000. "Ludwig M. Lachmann (1906-1990): Scholar, Teacher, and Austrian School Critic of Late Classical Formalism in Economics." *American Journal of Economics and Sociology*, 59(3):367–417.

Moss, Laurence S. (2005). "The applied economics of the modern Austrian School." In *Modern applications of Austrian thought*, edited by Jürgen G. Bakhaus, 3–19. London and New York: Routledge.

Nardi Spiller, Cristina. (1993). "Une analyse interprétative du modèle cyclique de Fanno." In *Rivista Internazionale di Scienze Economiche e Commerciali*, 40 (5):397–410.

Nardi Spiller, Cristina. (2000). "Affinità e distinguo nell'analisi delle fluttuazioni cicliche tra Fanno e Hayek." In *Nuova Economia e Storia*, 6 (1-2):73–94.

O'Driscoll, Gerald P., and Mario J. Rizzo. (1985). *The economics of time and ignorance*. London and New York: Routledge, 2002.

Phaneuf, Emile, and Carmelo Ferlito. (2014). "On human rationality and government control." In *Procesos de Mercado: Revista Europea de Economía Política*, 11 (2):137–181.

Pindyck, Robert S., and Daniel L. Rubinfeld. (2013). *Microeconomics*. Upper Saddle River: Pearson.

Prychitko, David L. (1994). "Ludwig Lachmann and the interpretative turn in economics: A critical inquiry into the hermeneutics of the plan." In *Advances in Austrian Economics*, 1, 303–319. London: JAI Press.

Prychitko, David L. (1995a). "Introduction: Why hermeneutics?" In *Individuals, institutions, interpretations. hermeneutics applied to economics*, edited by David L. Prychitko, 1–5. Aldershot, UK and Brookfield, US: Avebury.

Prychitko, David L., ed. (1995b). *Individuals, institutions, interpretations. hermeneutics applied to economics*. Aldershot, UK, Brookfield, US: Avebury.

Prychitko, David L. (2010). "Competing explanations of the Minsky moment: The financial instability hypothesis in the light of Austrian theory." *The Review of Austrian Economics*, 23:199–221.

Rizzo, Mario J. (1979). "Disequilibrium and all that: An introductory essay." In *Time, uncertainty, and disequilibrium: Exploration of Austrian themes*, edited by Mario J. Rizzo, 1–18. Lexington, D.C.: Heath and Company.

Rizzo, Mario J. (1992). "Equilibrium Visions." In *Modern Austrian Economics. Archaeology of a Revival*, Volume 2, *The Age of Dispersal*, edited by Peter J. Boettke, and Stephan Boehm, 175–190. London: Pickering & Chatto, Robinson 2002, Joan. (1974). "History versus Equilibrium." In *Collected economic papers*, V, by Joan Robinson, 48–58. Oxford: Basil Blackwell, 1979.

Rothbard, Murray N. (1962). "Man, economy, and state: A treatise on economic principles." In *Man, economy, and state: a treatise on economic principles with power and market. government and the economy*, by Murray N. Rothbard, 1–1046. Auburn: Ludwig von Mises Institute, 2004.

Rothbard, Murray N. (1969). *Economic depressions: Their cause and cure*. Auburn: Ludwig von Mises Institute, 2009.

Rothbard, Murray N. (1987). "Time preference." In *Pure-Time preference theory of interest*, edited by Jeffrey M. Herbener, 59–66. Auburn: Ludwig von Mises Institute, 2011.

Rothbard, Murray N. (1989). "The hermeneutical invasion of philosophy and economics." In *Economic controversies*, by Murray N. Rothbard, 119–136. Auburn: Ludwig von Mises Institute, 2011.

Rothbard, Murray N. (1992). "The present state of Austrian economics." In *Modern Austrian economics. Archaeology of a revival*, Volume 2, *The Age of Dispersal*, edited by Peter J. Boettke, and Stephan Boehm, 1–59. London: Pickering & Chatto, 2002.

Salerno, Joseph T. (2012). "A reformulation of Austrian business cycle theory in light of the financial crisis." *The Quarterly Journal of Austrian Economics*, 15(1):3–44. Retrieved from *https://mises.org/library/reformulation-austrian-business-cycle-theory-light-financial-crisis-0*.

Schumpeter, Joseph A. (1911). "The theory of economic development (1911).: The fundamental phenomenon of economic development." In *The entrepreneur: Classic texts by Joseph Schumpeter*, edited by Marcus C. Becker, Thorbjørn Knudsen, and Richard Swedberg, 79–154. Stanford: Stanford University Press, 2011.

Schumpeter, Joseph A. (1928). "The entrepreneur in today's economy." In *The entrepreneur: Classic texts by Joseph Schumpeter*, edited by Marcus C.

Becker, Thorbjørn Knudsen, and Richard Swedberg, 261–285. Stanford: Stanford University Press, 2011.

Schumpeter, Joseph A. (1934). *The theory of economic development: An inquiry into profits, capital, credit, interest, and the business cycle.* New Brunswick and London: Transaction Publishers, 1983.

Schumpeter, Joseph A. (1935). "The analysis of economic change." *The Review of Economics and Statistics*, 17(4):2–10.

Schumpeter, Joseph A. (1939). *Business cycles: A theoretical, historical, and statistical analysis of the capitalist process.* Retrieved from *http://classiques.uqac.ca/classiques/Schumpeter_joseph/business_cycles/schumpeter_business_cycles.pdf.*

Schumpeter, Joseph A. (1942). *Capitalism, socialism & democracy.* London and New York: Routledge, 2003.

Schumpeter, Joseph A. (1947). "The creative response in economic history." *The Journal of Economic History*, 7(2):149–159.

Schumpeter, Joseph A. (1954). *History of economic analysis.* London and New York: Routledge, 2006.

Schumpeter, Joseph A. (1964). *Business cycles. A theoretical, historical, and statistical analysis of the capitalist process.* 2008 abridged edition. Retrieved from *http://classiques.uqac.ca/classiques/Schumpeter_joseph/business_cycles/schumpeter_business_cycles.pd.*

Selgin, George A. (1988). *Praxeology and understanding: An analysis of the controversy in austrian economics.* Auburn: Ludwig von Mises Institute, 1990.

Shackle, George L.S. (1953). "What makes an economist?" In *Uncertainty in economics and other reflections*, by George Shackle, 241–257. New York and Cambridge, UK: Cambridge University Press, 2010.

Shackle, George L.S. 1965. *A scheme of economic theory.* New York and Cambridge, UK: Cambridge University Press.

Shackle, George L.S. (1972). *Epistemics and economics: A critique of economic doctrines.* New Brunswick and London: Transaction Publishers, 2009.

Solow, Robert M. (1956). "A contribution to the theory of economic growth." *Quarterly Journal of Economics*, 70(1):65–94.

Solow, Robert M. (1957). "Technical change and the aggregate production function." *Review of Economics and Statistics*, 39(3):312–320.

Spiethoff, Arthur. (1925). "Business Cycles." In *Business cycle theory: Selected texts 1860-1939*, Volume 2, *Structural Theories of the Business*

Cycle, edited by Harald Hagemann, 109–205. London: Pickering and Chatto, 2002.

Steele, G.R. (2001). *Keynes and Hayek. The money economy.* London and New York: Routledge.

Sylos Labini, Paolo. (1954). "Il problema dello sviluppo economico in Marx e Schumpeter." In *Problemi dello sviluppo economico*, by Paolo Sylos Labini, 19–73. Bari: Laterza, 1977.

Sylos Labini, Paolo. (1984). *The forces of economic growth and decline.* Cambridge, MA and London: MIT Press.

Vaughn, Karen. (1994). *Austrian economics in America. The migration of a tradition.* New York and Cambridge, UK: Cambridge University Press, 1998.

Wicksell, Knut. (1893). *Value, Capital and Rent.* London: George Allen & Unwin, 1954.

ABOUT THE AUTHOR

Carmelo Ferlito (Verona, Italy, 1978) is an Italian scholar who, since 2011, lives in Subang Jaya, Malaysia.

Since 2013 Carmelo Ferlito is an Adjunct Faculty Member at INTI International College Subang, Subang Jaya, Malaysia, where he teaches *History of Economic Thought* and *Microeconomic Theory and Policy* for the University of Wollongong Programme.

Since 2012 he is a Senior Fellow at the Institute for Democracy and Economic Affairs (IDEAS), a free-market think tank based in Kuala Lumpur, Malaysia.

In 2003 he earned a Master. in economics at the University of Verona (Italy), writing a dissertation on Schumpeter's business cycle theory under the guidance of Paolo Sylos Labini; the core of the thesis was published in 2011 by the *Quarterly Journal of Austrian Economics*. In 2007, he earned a Ph.D. in Economic History from the same university, producing a big work on the history of banking institutions, paying special attention to Monti di Pietà and ethical lending. The dissertation was published in 2009 by the prestigious Istituto Veneto di Scienze, Lettere e Arti in Venice. From 2004 to 2009 he cooperated as research fellow and teaching assistant with the chairs of economic history and history of economic thought of the University of Verona, the University of Macerata, and Salento University.

His research activity is presently devoted to develop Austrian economics. In particular he extended the Austrian approach to business cycles and capital theory, bringing forward what was done in the past by Friedrich A. von Hayek, Ludwig M. Lachmann, and Joseph A. Schumpeter.

Hermeneutics of Capital is Ferlito's fifth book. In total, he is the author of seven chapters in miscellaneous volumes, twenty-five articles published in scientific journals and about two hundred articles in newspapers and periodicals. In Italy, he has held about twenty conferences, while in Malaysia he has been invited to speak about the recession and economic fluctuations in about ten universities. His academic webpage is https://newinti.academia.edu/ CarmeloFerlito, where the full list of his publications can be found. Email: carmelo@uow.edu.au

INDEX

A

actual output, 33
adaptation, 66, 67, 74, 75, 78, 83
aggregate demand, 63
analytical framework, 4, 7, 45
assets, 62, 79
Austrian School, vii, xii, xvi, xvii, 1, 2, 35, 37, 43, 96

B

bankruptcies, 83
banks(ing), 37, 62, 63, 64, 68, 69, 73, 75, 82, 83, 84, 87, 101
business cycle, viii, ix, xi, 23, 37, 41, 51, 61, 64, 77, 83, 85, 86, 101
businesses, 40, 78

C

capital accumulation, 25
capital goods, vii, viii, xvi, 10, 12, 13, 14, 15, 16, 20, 21, 22, 23, 25, 31, 32, 57, 66, 71, 73, 77, 82, 85
capital stock, vii, 27
capitalism, 30, 31, 32, 33, 41
central bank, vii, ix, 59, 64, 67, 68, 74, 75, 79

circular flow, 36, 38, 42, 48, 49, 50, 75, 76
commodity, 8, 27, 37
competition, 29, 30, 33, 42, 43, 44, 51, 70
competitive advantage, 69, 77
competitive process, 35, 42, 44, 78
competitors, 40, 44
consumer choice, 69
consumer goods, vii, 64, 70, 71, 73, 77, 82, 83
consumers, 25, 36, 64, 65, 67, 70, 74, 75, 77, 79, 82, 83
consumption, vii, 10, 13, 15, 21, 25, 62, 63, 65, 70, 72, 75, 83, 86
consumption plans, vii
cost, xv, 24, 27, 29, 33, 72
currency, 63, 76
current account, 62
cycles, 61, 65, 66, 85, 86, 90
cyclical process, 85

D

debts, 73
disequilibrium, 2, 11, 23, 27, 29, 42, 47, 51, 67, 69, 70

social environment, 39, 41, 43
social phenomena, 2
socialism, 31, 33, 41
society, xv, 8, 22, 25, 37, 61, 76
South Africa, 1
Spain, xii
speculation, xii, xvii, 66, 70, 79, 85
state, xvi, 22, 27, 29, 33, 36, 39, 40, 42, 47, 51, 62, 78
stock, vii, 11, 12, 15, 27
structure, vii, xii, 11, 21, 22, 23, 24, 25, 26, 28, 65, 66, 67, 69, 70, 71, 74, 75, 78, 79, 80, 81, 83, 91
supply and demand, vii, 75
surplus, 27, 40
sustainable development, 37, 79, 80
sustainable growth, 79, 84

T

technological change, 54
technological progress, 54
technology, 43
trade, 64

transactions, 78
translation, 36

V

VPC, 17, 18, 19

W

wage rate, 68
wages, 62, 64, 70, 73, 76, 83
warlords, 41
Washington, xii
wealth, 2, 27, 30, 37
Wine barrels, vii
winery, vii
workers, 32, 76, 83

Y

yield, 25, 72